LLOYD NOLAN:
An Actor's Life With Meaning

Joel Blumberg & Sandra Grabman

Published in the USA by:
BearManor Media
P O Box 71426
Albany, Georgia 31708
www.bearmanormedia.com

Printed in the United States of America
ISBN 978-1-59393-600-6

Book and cover design by Darlene Swanson • www.van-garde.com

Contents:

To Biff Elliot

The first to play Mike Hammer.
Who thirty-two years ago befriended a young sportscaster
and cultivated his love of motion pictures

— Joel Blumberg

Acknowledgements

Our heartfelt thanks go to the wonderful people listed below for their generosity in sharing information and memories with us.

Lloyd's Family: Son-in-law Timothy Cairns, former son-in-law Don Lightfoot, grandson Nolan Lightfoot

Lloyd's Friends and Acquaintances: Harriet Dawkins, Marilyn Henry, Connie & Dr. Harvey Lapin, Stone Wallace

Lloyd's Peers in Field of Autism: Dennis & Carol Hansen, Connie & Dr. Harvey Lapin, Dr. Ruth Sullivan

Lloyd's Peers in the Entertainment Industry: Lynn Bari (through her biographer Jeff Gordon), Larry Cohen, Alex Cord, Michael B. Druxman, Anne Francis, Paul Gregory, Sybil Jason, Wright King, Don Murray, Roy Rowland (through his son Steve), Connie Stevens

Historians: Film historian Lon and Debra Davis, Gary Giddins, Marvin Paige's Motion Picture & TV Research Archives

Photos: Eleanor Knowles Dugan, Dr. Harvey Lapin, Don Lightfoot, Nolan Lightfoot, Julia Posel, Christina Rice/Los Angeles Public Library

Collectors: Robert Ligtermoet of Robert's Videos, Grace McKay

Research Assistance: Ancestry.com, Joanne Batziotegos, Tom Carey of the San Francisco History Center/San Francisco Public Library, Sheila Conway of the Santa Clara University Archives, Jeff Gordon, Klaus D. Haisch, Jenny Johnson of the Stanford University Archives, the Margaret Herrick Library in Los Angeles, Dr. Gary Mesibov, Frank Quaranti, Paul M. Quigley, Sylvia Rowan of the San Francisco Public Library, Larry Smith, Michael Schlossheimer, Chuck South-cott, Jeff Strully, Lynn Thacker of the Duncan Public Library, Nancy of Pennsylvania State University, Wikipedia and a special thanks to Ned Comstoc of the University of Southern California

Foreword

A fascinating biography of one of Hollywood's most depend
able, under appreciated stars. Lloyd Nolan was a steady hand
in countless movies and this book traces his roots and carries the
reader along on a journey through a bygone era of Hollywood, all the
while concentrating on the career of an actor who brought depth and
a back story to every one of his characters. A leading man, a supporting player and later a character actor were all roles he handled flaw-
lessly. The book goes into incredible detail about his life so that what
emerges is a rounded portrait of a solid Hollywood. star. It's invalu-
able for film historians or for movie fans who love great acting and
remember him with deep affection. "

Jeffrey Lyons
2010

Introduction

Lloyd Nolan first came into my consciousness when, in my youth, I watched him and Diahann Carroll each week on the television series *Julia*. His face was familiar, so I knew I'd seen him in other places, too.

Fast forward, then, to 2004, when I was researching the life and career of 1940s child star Peggy Ann Garner in preparation for writing her biography. While watching Peggy Ann in her Oscar-winning performance in *A Tree Grows in Brooklyn* (1945), I also noticed that Lloyd was playing the compassionate police officer with such tenderness that it left me wanting to see more of his work. Thank goodness for videotape and DVDs! His characters in *Airport* and *Earthquake* were exceptional. He was completely believable in *Peyton Place*. His work as the title character in *Michael Shayne, Private Detective* was a lighthearted treat. It had never occurred to me that he could do that sort of comedy. Career-wise, Lloyd Nolan certainly had my respect.

Then I learned of his tireless efforts to better the lives of people with autism and their families. That struck a chord with me. Like Lloyd, I have an autistic son. After more research, I learned that my son has personally benefited from the off-screen work that Lloyd did on our behalf. The man definitely deserves a biography.

WGBB radio host Joel Blumberg is a fount of knowledge about

and has much enthusiasm for vintage film and television. On his *Silver Screen Audio* show each week, he interviews an actor, writer, historian, or other such person who has new information on the subject for his listeners. When he interviewed me, I was very impressed with Joel's intelligent and knowledgeable questions. Add to that the fact that he very much admires Lloyd Nolan's work, and you've got a terrific co-author.

Consequently, we came up with an agreement: We would write Lloyd's biography together. Joel would share information about Lloyd's professional life, and I would focus on his personal life. We would each be doing what we do best, and this book is the result of this fine collaboration. I hope you enjoy it.

—Sandra Grabman, 2010

It could be argued that Lloyd Nolan was the most prolific actor of his time. There are people who look at his resume of ninety-four films and many more television shows and question the validity of that statement. They will point out that there are character actors that have appeared in more than three times Lloyd's output. Consider this. From his first film, Warner Bros.' "G"Men, Lloyd received billing in each one of his cinematic efforts, while those "characters" were screen-billed in less than half of their movies.

Lloyd Nolan could play any character in any genre and was believable in every role. I remember growing up in the Queens section of New York City, not far from the Astoria studios that Paramount Pictures owned, and every weekday at 5:30 PM watching a film series on WCBS Channel 2 called *The Early Show.* It was in the days where local channels owned the exclusive rights to show films from the studios. Channel 2 owned the early Paramounts and, because of this, I got to see many of Lloyd's films that are not available today due to Universal's reluctance to capitalize on the classic market by selling them on DVDs like Warner Home Video (Warner Bros, MGM, RKO, and Monogram), 20th Century-Fox, and Sony (Columbia). He impressed me as a real good guy even when he played a real bad guy. He was not acting; he was just real. He came off as a New Yorker, even though he was from San Francisco. I began to follow Lloyd's career and, as I got older, I really came to appreciate his lack of histrionics. He *was* Michael Shayne in those Fox films. He *was* Inspector Briggs in *The House on 92nd Street* and *The Street With No Name*. He *was* Dr. Swain in *Peyton Place* and, even as a bad guy; he *was* Lt. De Garmot in *Lady in the Lake*.

Too often you find that the celebrities you admire have led less than admirable lives off screen. Multiple marriages, arrests, cover-ups, and worse. It is the price of Hollywood. Yet, I never heard a bad word about Lloyd. A solid relationship with a wife he truly loved and vice versa. Two children. The antithesis of the typical Hollywood star.

When Sandy Grabman approached me about helping her write the story of Lloyd's life, I couldn't say yes fast enough. By this time I had known about autism and Lloyd's connection with it. It only made my respect for this man deeper.

I hope that when you read this collaboration you'll have the same respect for Lloyd that Sandy and I do.

—Joel Blumberg, 2010

CHAPTER 1
The Beginnings

It was 1902. This was the year that production-line automobiles came into being. Here in San Francisco, these newfangled cars would give stiff competition to the usual form of transportation—cable cars. Movies had been around for fourteen years, but were still silent. It would be a quarter century later before *The Jazz Singer* would introduce theatergoers to feature-length talkies. America's first movie theater, the Electric Theatre, opened its doors for the first time south of here, in Los Angeles.

Many of the babies born this year would make exceptional marks on the world—Tallulah Bankhead, Charles Lindbergh, Richard Rodgers, Victor Jory, and Margaret Hamilton. There was another very special baby, too. On Tuesday, August 11, Margaret Shea Nolan presented her husband, James Clair Nolan, with a baby boy. They named him Lloyd Benedict Nolan, and he came into the family when brother James Clair Jr. was eight and sister Estelle Marie was two.

Both of Lloyd's parents were of one hundred percent Irish stock. James, in fact, had been born in Ireland. He had immigrated to America with his family when he was a wee babe. Now he was a forty-three-year-old man with a wife and three children to support, but this was

America, where a man could earn a good living if he was willing to work hard. And a good living it was. James was a partner in Nolan & Company, his family's shoe-and boot-manufacturing business that was doing quite well.

The earliest memory Lloyd had of his childhood occurred when he was three. The family was abruptly woken in the early morning hours of April 18, 1906, to shaking and rumbling. It was the Great Earthquake, so violent that it could be felt from Oregon to Southern California, but was at its apex right here in San Francisco. Mr. and Mrs. Nolan gathered their family together and went outside, which was the first time Lloyd had ever seen his parents in their nightclothes. He remembered his

The devastated business district of San Francisco. Photos taken by George Lawrence from a series of kites five weeks after the Great Earthquake and fires.

mother then holding him, but she didn't have to soothe him. At such a tender age, he thought this rumbling new world was great fun.

It wasn't nearly as much fun for the adults, though. The quake had ruptured gas mains and water pipes, which caused fires throughout the city and left firefighters helpless to do much about them. So much damage was done by this catastrophe that vital records that had been maintained there were destroyed. Lloyd and his siblings would have to find some other proofs-of-birth in the future as their birth certificates were now reduced to ashes.

The Nolan home, at 1116 Fulton Street, escaped the fires, but Nolan & Company was not as fortunate. The business, originally located at 1308 Market Street, 516-518 Mission Street, and 7 McAllister in the Callighan Building, had been in the sections of town that suffered extensive fire damage. The company would come alive again

Lloyd's childhood home, as it looks today.

and, in 1910, would be renamed the Nolan-Earl Shoe Company. Its new location would be 24-25 Fremont Street.

Shoes and boots were needed by everyone and the Nolan family was known for their quality products, so James was able to support his family in style. According to the 1910 census, they had two live-in servants—an Irish maid named Delia Bully and an Oriental cook named Yee Quong Ye.

Lloyd would someday tell his grandson anecdotes that would indicate that the man had been quite a handful as a boy. When someone knocked at the front door, young Lloyd liked to slide all the way down from the top floor on the banister and answer the door. Playing cowboy was a favorite pastime for him, perhaps having been influenced by the 1903 film *The Great Train Robbery*; and the household servants would sometimes be on the receiving end of a lasso as they came up the backstairs. This once came close to causing a tragedy when the lasso settled around the neck of Yee Quong Ye and he lost his balance, falling off the stairs. A couple of maids had quit, in fact, because of the antics of the youngest Nolan.

Sometimes, Lloyd was the victim, rather than the perpetrator. It became almost a yearly occurrence for him to come home with a black eye, which they then treated with leeches. (Perhaps it was this "leech treatment" that formed the root of Lloyd's extreme distaste as an adult for all things medical.) He also had to have his stomach pumped once because his big brother had talked him into eating a mud pie. Boys will be boys, eh?

As he grew, Lloyd developed a fondness for playing pool and riding his homemade I-shaped vehicle down hills, with his feet serving as its brakes. San Francisco is a very hilly city, and one had to walk

Young Lloyd on the right, unidentified friend on the left.
(From the collection of Nolan Lightfoot)

Silhouette of thirteen-year-old Lloyd, shown by his friend Harvey Lapin.
(Courtesy of the Lapin family)

uphill to get to the Nolan home, so there were plenty of places to ride that little car.

At the age of thirteen, Lloyd rose victorious in the *San Francisco Examiner* newspaper's Animal Story Contest. There had been four-hundred-eighty-nine entries in his age division; and his story, entitled "My Pets," was awarded second prize. The resulting article in the Sunday, November 28, 1915, edition of the newspaper featured a solemn-faced photo of Lloyd, dressed immaculately in a suit and holding his black dog. He would love dogs throughout his life.

Lloyd's mother, on the other hand, loved theatre entertainment and would oftentimes take him with her to see the shows of visiting stars. When those stars were from San Francisco, it wasn't unusual for her to already know them personally. Margaret had wanted to act on stage in a major way, but that had never worked out for her. This, Lloyd felt later, was when he first began thinking of acting as a career possibility for himself.

As the years passed, Lloyd gained new skills.

Family legend is that the Nolans were the second family in San Francisco to own a car. Dad James did not know how to drive and brother Clair had his own home and family (while still working as buyer/manager for Nolan-Earl Shoe Company), so Lloyd did the chauffeuring. It wasn't easy, either. Their city was often very foggy. When that happened, friends would sit on the hood, chew tobacco, then spit its juice onto the windshield to make the moisture slide off. Apparently, that didn't remedy the situation entirely because they still had to let Lloyd know when it was time to make a turn.

Clair would later become a career Navy man. Would young Lloyd be the one to take over the family business, James wondered.

CHAPTER 2
Glorious Youth

In 1918, at the age of sixteen, Lloyd left the comfort of San Francisco and entered the University of Santa Clara High School's Preparatory Department, on the University campus in Santa Clara. Prep school and college were routinely combined in this era. He attended this school for four years and lived on campus. This appears to have been a halfway-type college, encompassing the last two years of high school and the first two years of college.

During his first year at SCU, Lloyd took Latin, English, religion, first-year algebra, and ancient history. It is not unusual for first-year students to have their plate full just attending to their classes as they adjust to life away from home. Nevertheless, Lloyd found time to participate in the April 8, 1919, Elocution Contest for Owl and Junior Prizes in which he orated *Fagin in Prison*, by Charles Dickens. He won second prize, which was ten dollars.

His classes the second year were Latin, English, religion, plane geometry, and modern and medieval history. Lloyd again participated in a contest. He received First Honors in Elocution and English Composition, meaning he was the top student in his class who had a yearly average of eighty-five percent or higher. The medal he won was later lost in a fight.

During the summer when school was out, Lloyd worked in his family's shoe business. James wanted very much for his sons to be a permanent part of the company, but that was definitely not in Lloyd's area of interest. Shoemaking was fine for others, but he wanted to go a different route. To please his father, though, he served as secretary to the business.

Back to school he went.

Lloyd began his third year at Santa Clara. The 1920 census indicates that, while Lloyd was living on campus with ninety-eight other young men, his older sister Estella was still living at home, and they no longer had any servants. Apparently, putting a son through college, as well as the recession of 1920, required some belt tightening.

During this year, Lloyd took Latin, English, religion, second-year algebra, and the history of England. He entered the Oratorical and Elocution Contests for the Owl and Junior Prizes again on April 27, 1920, performing *The Maniac*, and won the fifteen-dollar first prize. He also again took First Honors in Elocution, Second Honors in English Composition, and the Distinguished designation in English Literature. It seems to have been in this year that Lloyd answered the siren call of the stage. He entered the Dramatic Art Contest on March 18, 1921, and played the lead role in the love-tale of a Texas Ranger. For this, he won the first prize, which was a gold watch and chain worth $200. One of the judges, Father Murphy, wrote in *University Notes* that Lloyd won that award for "general brilliance." He wrote, in part, "he was very graceful, very earnest, with a real, sympathetic quality in all he did; and he moved around with a degree of grace and freedom that made us feel that we could see him do it all over once more." The following month, Lloyd did the introductory in the Annual Contest in Public Speaking for the Owl and Junior Prizes.

Among his fellow stage-bound students of SCU over the years were Andy Devine, Jackie Coogan, and Edmund Lowe. The school's theatre was affectionately called The Ship. It served as both theatre and dormitory, and its backstage walls were covered with its players' signatures. Lloyd painted his "Tub Nolan" nickname way up high on that wall where no one could reach. How did he do it? Future son-in-law Don Lightfoot solved the mystery when he revealed that Lloyd "was held by his feet by friends." He continues, "As an adult, and a celebrity, he was asked to speak at this school. The headmaster (or priest) took him up to the bell tower to show him that his name [was] still there." Sadly, The Ship would ultimately become a fire hazard and was demolished in the summer of 1962.

(Courtesy of Santa Clara
University Archives)

He was a member of the Junior Debating Society, which was having some difficulty attracting new members. Thus, they appointed a committee to take care of that problem. Lloyd was not only chosen to be on that committee, but he was also the Society's reporter. On May 3, 1921, they competed with San Jose High School's debaters on the topic "Resolved, That the United States should recognize the independence of the Philippine Islands during the Present Administration." Lloyd and three other students were chosen to represent SCU at this competition, and they were declared the victors by a unanimous vote of the judges.

The preparatory students of SCU formed a group called Associated Students of the Preparatory Department of the University of Santa Clara, and they elected Lloyd as its president. Part of his responsibilities was to work with a committee to draw up a constitution. The preparatory students would no longer be part of the College Department, regarding parliamentary matters and athletic activities, but would be a separate entity, though they would still be a part of the University in spirit. This would give the preparatory students more say over parliamentary issues.

Then Lloyd began his fourth year at SCU; and his subjects were Latin, English, religion, first-semester solid geometry, second-semester plane trigonometry, first-semester civics, and second-semester U.S. history. In spite of his full schedule, he still had time to win First Honors in Elocution and receive the Distinguished honors in English Literature and Composition. He continued the extracurricular work he had begun earlier, and seems to have also played the lead in the school drama *The Bells* in this year.

No slouch was Lloyd Benedict Nolan at USC, except . . .

Physics was a prerequisite for entering the Engineering program, and Greek was required in the third and fourth years for those who desired to work toward their Bachelor of Arts degree. Lloyd had no use for those things. He knew now what he wanted to do with his life. He wanted to act.

In 1922, he began his studies at Stanford University and became a member of Delta Kappa Epsilon. His major was English, and a career as a newspaper journalist was his goal. Football, too, looked inviting.

Lloyd inherited his mother's love of acting.
(Courtesy of the Santa Clara University Archives)

Should he try out for the team? His cousin strongly advised him not to do it, because he had been seriously injured in the game. Nevertheless, Lloyd participated on the team as freshman fullback. He did not get a lot of play time, however; not because of any injury, but because teammate Ernie Nevers was a better fullback.

Even though Lloyd was not a senior, he was given the lead in the senior play that year. This led to membership in The University Players, a theatrical group that staged twelve plays a year. Unfortunately, his first play at Stanford took place at exam time.

While Lloyd was busy with plays, the womenfolk back home were achieving some notoriety of their own. Estella was listed in the prestigious *Who's Who Among the Women of California* publication's 1922 edition, and their mom was listed in the *City & County Federation of Women's Clubs Yearbook, San Francisco 1918-1920*. Estella would never marry, and lived for many years in the family home.

Lloyd spent so much of his time doing the work involved in the school's plays that he neglected his studies and flunked out of Stanford. The rules were that one had to wait a year before reapplying to the school, so he and a fraternity brother took jobs on a world-cruise liner, working for the founder of Lockheed. In an interview published in the March, 1937, issue of *Modern Screen* magazine, Lloyd described his job on that liner as

> an understudy to an officer, at a salary of twenty-five cents a month. At least, that's what it seemed like. And it took tall talking to get the job. The liner had had too much experience with young cubs who quit after the first trip. Which, by the way, was what we intended to do.

It was hard work, for sure, but they had great times when the ship docked. Lloyd would later meet a friend's father-in-law whose youth had been spent in much the same way. They would compare notes; not only about their travels, but also about the bordellos they visited.

While ashore in Singapore, Lloyd excitedly spent his entire pay on some beautiful emeralds for his mother. Much later, after he returned to the States with them, he would learn that he had been scammed. They were only green glass. Still beautiful, but worth very little.

They had gone almost all the way around the world on this ship when it docked in New York. Lloyd and his buddy got dressed up in regular clothes and went to a show on shore. When they returned shortly before midnight, they were the first to notice that the ship was on fire. "I rushed on board," he said, "and waved an empty hose around for about ten minutes, until I cracked wise that something was wrong with the water pressure; then headed for shore, along with a cloud of smoke."

So there they were on shore with only $3.36 between them. What to do? Time for some more of that tall talking. It worked! For $3.00, they got an entire suite in the Hotel McAlpin. "We tipped the bellhop a quarter with a grand gesture, and had eleven cents left."

Luckily, his friend's mother came and rescued them the following morning. The liner offered to let them work their way back to San Francisco on one of their freighters. Lloyd had heard about freighter food, so, instead, wired his parents, "Miscalculated financial status by about five thousand miles. Please send money."

It was just a few weeks after Lloyd's return home that his father died. No longer did he have a benevolent patriarch to smooth his way in life. He would now have to become completely self-sufficient.

The family business, too, felt the loss deeply. The firm would later be liquidated.

Lloyd and a former Stanford classmate decided to do a vaudeville routine, with Lloyd as the stooge. They worked killer hours, and it was difficult to come up with new material as often as they needed to, so they gave up that line of work after four months.

By now, the required year had passed, and Lloyd was free to re-enter Stanford. He worked his way through with whatever jobs he could find, including waiting tables at the fraternity house and punching tickets at sporting events. Back in the leading roles at the campus theatre, he was able to feel important at least some of the time.

It was here at Stanford that Lloyd appeared in his very first movie. It was the story of Stanford, entitled *Stanford Days,* written by and played by undergraduate students. He played the part of the athlete. "And was I hammy!" he told the *Modern Screen* reporter. His acting style would improve in the years to come.

A star student Lloyd wasn't. He aced English, which was supposed to be difficult, but had an aversion to a course that was supposed to be easy, chemistry. The lab reeked of what seemed to him to be medicinal odors; he had no good feelings about the course whatsoever, and made F's in it. President Lyman Wilbur couldn't understand this enigma, and suggested he just become an actor.

By the 1925-1926 year, Lloyd had earned eighty-four Lower Division credits, but had now flunked out for the second time. He would not go back but, instead, decided to pursue his true calling, which had been tugging at his sleeve all along.

CHAPTER 3

Treading the Boards from Coast To Coast

Like most thespians, Lloyd did not just show up in Hollywood. The career that took him to every major studio and many of the minor ones took the usual circuitous route covering both US coasts.

With his Stanford University days behind him, Lloyd went south to the famous Pasadena Playhouse, where he would meet another young actor named Victor Jory. To Lloyd, this was his first litmus test. As he told *New York Journal American* columnist Dorothy Kilgallen, "My father had left me a couple of thousand dollars, so I came down to Pasadena to the playhouse, to see if I could really act. I knew college theatricals were no test. No matter how lousy you are in a college play, it's all right. Everybody thinks you're great."

Possessing a letter of introduction to the great Walter Hampden, he could have fast-tracked his way to success. Armed with the document, Lloyd gave it some thought, and then put it in his back pocket. "I never used it," Lloyd told Kilgallen, "because working with Walter Hampden was like working in a ditch. You never get anywhere." Lloyd's instinct proved correct. Hampden, known as a great Shakespearian actor, was also known as a scene stealer, as proven by his "Oliver Larrabee" characterization in Billy Wilder's *Sabrina* (in this case to good advantage as star Humphrey Bogart let him steal each scene the pair appeared in).

The first thing he did was a drama called *Aristocracy*, a chestnut that dated back to the 1890s. Playing Lloyd's young wife in the play was Mrs. Guy Bates Post, whose actual age was near seventy years. Despite the incongruity in casting, Lloyd found that he could act a little.

He would do twenty-two more plays before deciding to head to New York and Broadway.

At the Pasadena Playhouse, Lloyd was hired as a leading man, but one worked there without pay. There were many retired opera stars in his midst. He was able to earn some money on the side, however, when he worked for a short time with Edward Everett Horton's stock company's production of *The Queen's Husband*. For the first time, Lloyd was playing a bad-guy role, a revolutionist. It was during his time at the Playhouse and with the stock company that he was acting with pros, and he realized he could hold his own. Acting would, indeed, be a viable career for him.

When his year at the Playhouse was up, he was urged to come back to the family business and fill the void that his father's death had created. He didn't really want to, so set about making it obvious to those around him that he had no talent for the business world. It worked! He was asked to leave before running the Nolan-Earl Shoe Company into the ground. While feigning displeasure at the rejection, Lloyd secretly rejoiced and sent his trunks to New York City.

It was 1928. He went to join his trunks. All he needed was one chance, he felt, and the powers-that-be would see that he could do the job. It took years for his big break to come but, in the meantime,

Lloyd went to Chicago to join the road company of *The Front Page*, playing the role of Kruger in the Ben Hecht-Charles MacArthur classic, which starred Lee Tracy as Hildy Johnson and Osgood Perkins as Walter Burns. Other future Hollywooodites in the cast were Allen Jenkins, Eduardo Ciannelli, Willard Robertson and Joseph Calleia, who originated the role of Kruger. Lloyd got the part because of what was perceived as a physical resemblance to Calleia, the perception perhaps not accurate, but beneficial to him.

Others who would play this part were Matt Moore in the Lewis Milestone 1931 film version and Allen Garfield in Billy Wilder's 1974 film version. Regis Toomey was a modified version of the character, this time named Sanders, in Howard Hawks' *His Girl Friday*. On Broadway, Pat Harrington Sr. played Kruger in a 1945 revival that starred Lew Parker and Arnold Moss as Johnson and Burns. Conrad Janis played Kruger in a 1969 production, which starred Robert Ryan and Bert Convy as Burns and Johnson.

During the Chicago run, Lloyd was staying in a hotel down the block from where the St. Valentine's Day Massacre was taking place. He was unaware of the murders until a day or two afterward. Once he was told, he was quite shaken by it.

From Chi-town to Cleveland for some more stock work. According to Dorothy Kilgallen's *New York Journal American* column, the reason Lloyd wound up moving scenery instead of acting at the Dennis Theater in Cape Cod in 1928 was because he had suddenly tired of acting.

Perhaps Miss Kilgallen was mistaken about that, for it was in that same year that Lloyd made a guest appearance as Paraclete in Stanford University's play *The Chief Thing*. Perhaps, at Cape Cod, he was merely supporting other actors for a while.

Also in the Theater's employ was a young ticket taker from Lowell, Massachusetts, named Ruth Elizabeth Davis. She would soon leave the box office and graduate to the stage. She then changed her first name to Bette.

Off hours, Lloyd spent a great deal of time on the beach. Little did he know that this simple part of his daily routine would lead him back to the footlights as a singing and dancing pirate in a 1929 production called *The Cape Cod Follies*. To John Vargara, in his October 26, 1954, *Personalities in the News* article entitled "Quietly the Captain Waited," Lloyd recalled getting the job "because I had the best tan of any member of the cast." As was evident, Lloyd didn't take himself very seriously. The Shuberts liked the show so much they took it and a few of its actors, including Lloyd, to Broadway. He had made it to the big time! A stage actor could hardly do better than Broadway. One of his fellow cast members was a very young Bette Davis. They would become good friends. The twenty-eight-scene revue opened on September 18, 1929, and ran for twenty-nine performances.

Lloyd would stay in New York, work in places like Brooklyn and New Jersey, suburban neighbors to Gotham, but still wanted to return to the Great White Way.

There's a comedy he might try called *Sweet Stranger*, suggested a stage-director friend. Try he did, and they liked him so much that, unbeknownst to Lloyd, they ousted another actor so he could play the part of an office boy. Apparently not realizing that he was going to be physically close to anyone that day, Lloyd had had onions for lunch prior to the first rehearsal.

As luck would have it, he *would* have close encounters with someone—22-year-old Mell Efird, a Columbia law student who was playing the part of a stenographer.

Mary Mell Efird was a proper southern lady whose ancestors had emigrated from Germany and settled in the Carolinas. Her mother had died when Mell was very young, so she was raised by her beloved father. Father and daughter were very close. She would have had the distinction of being the first female in North Carolina to graduate from law school, had her father not died in her senior year at Columbia. Mell was then on her own. While at North Carolina Woman's College, then again in New York, she had studied the art of drama.

With her innate sense of justice, Mell was immediately resentful of Lloyd, not only because of his onion-breath, but also because he had taken another man's role. That wasn't fair. Lloyd had a different kind of feeling for her, though. He gallantly walked her home after each rehearsal and performance, and her feelings for him softened.

For the only time in his long career, Lloyd was billed as Lloyd B. Nolan. Staged by future television pioneer Worthington Minor, the play opened at the Cort Theater in October of 1930. *Sweet Stranger* lasted only twenty-four performances, but the relationship that was formed in that production would last a lifetime. Off-stage life imitated art. In the play, Lloyd's character fell in love with Mell's. Now Lloyd was falling in love with Mell Efrid. The way the play was structured, Lloyd and Mell had plenty of time for romance. "Mel and I were in the first and third act," recalled Lloyd to *New Yorker* reporter Emory Lewis, "that gave us the second act to get our romancing in."

Now the play was over. What's next?

Almost another year passed before Lloyd would find Broadway work. This time he was moved into a higher rent district, thanks once again to Worthington Minor, who gave Lloyd an almost-juvenile role of Emil, who learns about Psychology in George Bernard Shaw's *Re-*

union in Vienna, starring the greatest husband-and-wife team in theater history, Alfred Lunt and Lynn Fontanne. The play, which was one of Shaw's least-known, concerned an Austrian Prince (Lunt) who was forced into exile, becoming a taxi driver in Nice, and his former love (Fontanne) now married to a successful psychiatrist (Minor Watson). The marriage is troubled by the wife's constant measuring of her husband to her old flame. When the psychiatrist learns that the former prince has now returned to Vienna, he suggests she meet up with her ex-beau so he could see how much more positive her life is. The reviews of the play were mixed, but the drawing power of the Lunts made it a success. *Reunion in Vienna* opened at the Martin Beck in July of 1932 and lasted for two hundred sixty-four performances. MGM would buy the screen rights to the play and put it on the screen in 1933, starring John Barrymore and Diana Wynyard, with Frank Morgan as the psychiatrist. Recreating their stage roles were Henry Travers, making his film debut as the psychiatrist's father, and Eduardo Ciannelli.

For his work in this play, Lloyd received $60 per week, which was considered good money during the Great Depression. Having a role in such a successful play gave him security, and he and Mell were talking about getting married, but Lloyd didn't feel that he was financially stable enough to do that yet.

How did Lloyd handle it when he didn't agree with a play's director about how he should play a scene? "I have learned not to argue," he admitted to a reporter of *The San Francisco Chronicle,* "to do what the director wants at rehearsals and then on the first night to act a scene the way it seems to me it should be acted."

When *Reunion* closed, Lloyd secured work in another musical revue called *Americana,* also known as *The Third American.* He had two totally diverse parts in the revue. In one number he played Button the Banker, a good guy. In another he was Nails Malarky, a gangster, Public Enemy 1-10 Inclusive. This was the first time Lloyd had played a villain, although a humorous one, on Broadway. Among those credited for the music were Harold Arlen and E.Y. Harburg, who later combined for the magnificent score of *The Wizard of Oz*, and Herman Hupfield, who wrote "As Time Goes By," made famous by the immortal *Casablanca*. The signature song of the show, sung by Lloyd, was the perfect anthem for the time: "Brother, Can You Spare a Dime?" The show ran for seventy-seven performances.

In five short years, Lloyd Nolan had risen from stock-company player to legitimate actor and had built up quite a resume. He had met the girl of his dreams. Life was good.

It would soon get better.

CHAPTER 4
One Sunday Afternoon

Lloyd Nolan was acquiring a good reputation as an actor. Every new stop was a step up for the thirty-year-old Californian. Having completed the run of his third play in December of 1932, Lloyd was once again seeking employment. He wouldn't have to wait long. The country, in the midst of the Great Depression, was looking for escapism, and one of the best forms of escapism had been *Americana*.

Actor James Hagan was a member of the husband-wife team E.H. Sothern and Julia Marlowe's acting company. Known primarily for their Shakespearian presentations, the company utilized Hagan in productions of *Twelfth Night, The Taming of the Shrew* and *The Merchant of Venice*, in the late teens and early twenties. Hagan had acting jobs in other productions, but he felt that he might give writing a try. His first play was called *Guns*. The three-act play was set in two speakeasies, one in New York and one in Chicago, then finishing up somewhere along the Mexican Border. The play opened on Broadway in August on 1928 and closed forty-eight performances later.

Not deterred by this failure, Hagan decided to set his next play in small-town America. It was the story of Biff Grimes, a dentist who was in love with the beautiful Virginia Brush. His rival, Hugo Barnstead, framed Biff for a crime that sent him to prison, stole Virginia, and eventually married her. Biff married the plain Amy Lind. The years pass, and Hugo comes to Biff to get an emergency extraction. A still-bitter Biff plans to kill Hugo with an overdose of gas. Things change when Biff sees that Virginia has become an overbearing shrew, making Hugo's life miserable. Biff now realizes that the quality of his life is much better than it would have been had he married Virginia. Biff performs the extraction, but gets some measure of revenge by doing the job without giving Hugo gas.

The play was to be staged by Leo Bulgakov. He had seen Lloyd's work on the stage and wanted to offer him a part, but not the lead. Buglakov's agent found Lloyd munching on a doughnut on the patron side of a Broadway theater. Lloyd recalled in an article written for the MGM publication *The Lion's Roar* in 1942, "Things couldn't have been worse. It was during the Depression. Roles for characters were as scarce as new tires are today. Leslie Spiller and Leo Bulgakov asked me to play the 'heavy' in the production.

"I read the lines in a dentist's office. It was the only room they could afford to rent. During that time Spiller sat in the chair, I went through the part. Byron Shores had been temporarily set for the lead, but they gave it to me. I convinced them that I resembled Shores and had more experience."

One Sunday Afternoon was produced on a shoestring. Six weeks were spent on rehearsals. During that time the cast was always two weeks behind on their salaries. They didn't know from day to day if they were going to be able to hire a theater. Sometimes the cast rehearsed in a school gymnasium or a hotel room. Finally, "The Little Theater" was booked

Even with a major star to draw patrons, and the monetary issues temporarily taken care of by the February 15, 1933, opening night, the prospects for Lloyd and *One Sunday Afternoon* still looked bleak. To make matters worse, the reviews were overshadowed by an event taking place some thousand miles to the south, in Miami Beach, where President Franklin D. Roosevelt was riding in an open-top car. A man named Giuseppe Zangara attempted an assassination of Roosevelt, but his shot missed the President and struck Anton Cermak, the mayor of Chicago, who was sitting next to Mr. Roosevelt. Cermak never recovered from the shooting and died some three weeks later.

The production was marked by an absence of marquee names. Nolan as Biff was on stage for all but five minutes. Rankin Mansfield was Hugo, Mary Holsman was Virginia, and Francesca Bruning was Amy. The only other recognizable name was Percy Helton, who made a Hollywood career with his high-pitched voice and hunched-back posture.

When the reviews came out, though, Lloyd was praised for his work. Writing in *Gotham Live*, Vera Caspary, in her pre-*Laura* days, was a witness to the birth of Lloyd Nolan, star. "To the first night audience, he was still a young man of no importance. They watched cynically. When the play opened the first act was still too long and the audience moved around in their seats. But the curtain fell on a good scene and the applause was plentiful. The second act on *One Sunday Afternoon* is dramatic. And then came the pathetic, lovely homecoming in Act Three, the exquisite, harsh lovemaking, the inarticulate tenderness. The audience cried frankly.

"When the curtain fell, the audience stood in the aisles. They called the young man's name, they cheered and shouted. And the next morning the papers were filled with the praise of Lloyd Nolan, who had become a young man of importance."

One Sunday Afternoon was a hit, but there was still a money problem. FDR had hastily called a bank holiday and money to pay overdue bills could not be obtained. The show shut down for a week until finances could be resolved.

The play would be the only one that James Hagen would write. It ran for three-hundred-twenty-two performances, a remarkable run for a play in the midst of the Depression. But audiences took to this slice of America drama and this young man who dominated the proceedings. In the end a production that had as an auspicious start as this one, came within one vote from winning a Pulitzer Prize.

It was during one of the performances that one of the high points of Lloyd's life occurred. Since childhood, he had idolized San Francisco-bred actor David Warfield. The man was right there, sitting in the third row, he was told. "I was thrilled to my soul," Lloyd said to the *San Francisco Chronicle*. "At the end of the act when I had a call, I looked and saw him, a quiet, little old man .... I bowed to him and to the audience. After the next act I bowed to him again. He stood up and bowed to me, putting his hands up and applauding. That was a great moment."

The story would go to Hollywood almost immediately. Fredric March had read the play and thought it would make a good story for Gary Cooper. He told fellow Paramount contract player Coop about it and Coop urged Paramount to purchase the property. It had to be flattering for Lloyd to learn that Cooper, the studio's top ranking star, would assume the role of Biff and Fay Wray, coming off her triumph in *King Kong,* would portray Virginia. Neil Hamilton, who one day would play the role of Commissioner Gordon in the *Batman* TV series, played Hugo. Frank Tuttle was scheduled to direct, but left the film due to creative differences. Stephen Roberts took over the reins and received directorial credit.

That was not all for this property. Warner Bros. got the rights and tailored it for James Cagney in 1941, calling it *The Strawberry Blonde.* Rita Hayworth played Virginia, Olivia de Havilland was Amy, and Jack Carson was Hugo. Cagney's brother William produced the film and Raoul Walsh directed. By this time Lloyd was established in Hollywood but was not considered for the role of Biff, even though he was freelancing at the time and had done recent work at the studio. Lloyd was very friendly with William Cagney, who had appeared with Lloyd in his second film, *Stolen Harmony*; and his relationship with Jimmy went back to his first picture, *"G" Men*, where Lloyd played a supporting role. In preparing for the role, Jimmy would often go over to the Nolans' house to get some tips on how to play Biff, though the finished product had Biff more suited to Cagney's on-screen pugnacious personality.

In 1947, Walsh remade the story using the original title, but adding a music score and Technicolor to the proceedings. Dennis Morgan was Biff, Don DeFore was Hugo, Janis Paige was Virginia, and Dorothy Malone was Amy. Even with all of the new bells and whistles added to the screenplay, the film tanked.

The story continued to draw interest from the new television medium. A 1949 version of the *Ford Theater* featured Francesca Brunning, who played Amy in the original stage version, reprising her role for the small screen. Also featured in the cast were Hume Cronyn and Burgess Meredith. Two years later, another television production featured Richard Carlson, Virginia Gilmore and June Lockhart. The following year another TV version spotlighted Jack Warden as Biff, and yet another version a year later had Frank Albertson as Biff. In 1957, the *Lux Video Theater* had the interesting casting of the husband-and-wife teams of Peter Lind Hayes and Mary Healy playing opposite Gordon and Sheila MacRae. The irony of the casting was that Gordon MacRae played Biff and Mary Healy played Amy, while Peter Lind Hayes was Hugo and Sheila MacRae was Virginia. The show got one more shot in 1959, reverting to title of *The Strawberry Blonde* with David Wayne as Biff

Once the play had established its "hit" status, Lloyd finally felt that he would be able to support Mell, so they decided this would be a good time to get married. It would be romantic to elope, they thought; but practicality took priority over such notions. They were married at St. Mark's Church in the Bowery on May 23, 1933. Mell and her "Nolie" would be together for the rest of her life.

Don Lightfoot shows us another side of the Nolans:

> Henry was the Nolans' gardener for many years before WWII broke out. One day Henry [who was Japanese] came to their door and explained that he and his family were being sent to a "relocation camp" within 48 hours and if they knew anyone that would like to buy his equipment it would help him out. The Nolans purchased Henry's equipment. After the war, Henry came to the house and said that he did not want to take anyone's job, but if they were ever looking for another gardener, he would like to work for them. Mell said, "Start tomorrow." Henry explained that he could not start the next day because he didn't have any equipment. Lloyd and Mell took Henry to their garage where they had stored all of Henry's equipment since they purchased it from him. They *gave* it back to him as a "homecoming" gift and Henry was back in business. Henry maintained their

On the back of this photo is written "Mell Efird and Lloyd Nolan just after
marriage on May 23, 1933. We were married at St. Marks on the Bowery."
Photographer Maurice Coldberg. (From the collection of Nolan Lightfoot)

yard once every week as their gardener but came to the house early on trash day and returned later that day to put the trash cans away every week until he passed away in the late 1960s. Mell or Lloyd never had to move a trash can for twenty years. Henry's way of saying "thank you" for their kindness.

Mell and Lloyd always had the best-looking lawns and garden in the area. [Of Henry's passing, he says] It was a very sad loss of a dear, old friend.

Their next gardener would have a personality that was very different from Henry's:

When Henry died, Mell let the news out to friends that they needed a new gardener. She interviewed many but none seemed to be right. One day an old-country Italian man came for the interview. Mell was surprised that the man seemed to be interviewing her instead of her interviewing him. She confronted him with her feelings. He agreed with her and explained that he was looking for a place to keep his prize azaleas and that he would take care of the gardens if he could bring them over to "live" at their home. Mell agreed and had the most beautiful azalea bushes and trees all around the yard and pool. I don't think she ever let many people know that it was not her green thumb that made her yard so beautiful.

CHAPTER 5
Hollywood

When *One Sunday Afternoon* closed in December, 1933, Lloyd knew he would not be unemployed long. He was a Broadway star, newly married, and knew at that point that he would never again have to sit outside a producer's office.

Curiously, Lloyd chose a play by Bertram Millhauser, a veteran screenwriter who would go on to write several of the Universal Sherlock Holmes entries in the forties, and Beulah Marie Dix called *Ragged Army*. The cast included Roy Roberts, Philip Van Zandt and Forrest Taylor, who all would become well-known Hollywood character actors. The play should have been called *Ragged Production*. It was put out of its misery after all of two performances.

Lloyd's final fling on the boards before heading west was for the Group Theater. This was a curious match-up. The Theater was formed in 1931 by Harold Clurman, Cheryl Crawford and Lee Strasberg. Others involved in the group included Franchot Tone, John Garfield, Lee J. Cobb, Howard Da Silva, Will Geer, Elia Kazan and the brother-sister combination of Luther and Stella Adler. Members of the Group tended to hold left-wing political views and wanted to produce plays that dealt with important social issues. In addition, the Group also

Lloyd Nolan in *Ragged Army*, 1934. Photographer Ben Pinchot.

was a proponent of a style of acting developed by the Russian director Konstantin Stanislavsky, which relied on actors training a performance based on an inner emotional experience. It was called Method Acting. Many members of the Group were later investigated by the House UnAmerican Activities Committee. Some, like Kazan, Cobb and author Clifford Odets, were called to testify and named names. Others, like Garfield, Stella Adler, Da Silva and Will Geer, refused and were blacklisted. *Gentlewoman's* cast included Stella Adler, Roman Bohnen and Morris Carnovsky. While Lloyd was not vocal in his political beliefs, the mixing of his instinctive style of performing and the others' Method style seemed incongruous. That issue had to be a minor one, solved quickly, when the play closed after a dozen showings.

Movie scouts had taken notice of Lloyd's fine work, and offers began coming in. Just as quickly Lloyd turned them down. The live stage was where he wanted to be. But then when the next two plays, *Ragged Army* and *Gentlewoman*, lasted two days and two weeks respectively, those movie offers began looking pretty good. After turning down the role of a surgeon in the stage version of *Men in White* because of his aversion to hospitals, he decided to accept an offer from Paramount Pictures.

Of all the studios in Hollywood, it was felt that Paramount had an advantage in recruiting Broadway talent. They had studios built over in Astoria, Queens, just across the East River from Manhattan. They were able to recruit talent from the Theater. Many Broadway performers would do film work in the afternoon and stage work at night. The Marx Bros. made their first two films, *The Cocoanuts* and *Animal Crackers*, at the Astoria studios and did on-stage material, much of which would be used in subsequent plays the same night. The studio still exists today at 34-10 36th Street in Astoria. For years it was the home of radio station WFAN, the one-time home of "Imus in the Morning."

Thus, while Paramount still did the majority of its filming in California, they had more filmmaking people on the east coast than the others. It was easier for Paramount to see a star born on Broadway and sign him up.

Lloyd signed their contract to begin July 15, 1934, and Paramount brought Lloyd and Mell to California. The Nolans treated his pre-work time as a vacation and went to visit his hometown, San Francisco.

They needn't have hurried through that vacation. For six months, Lloyd sat idle, collecting a salary while doing nothing. He then free-lanced a bit and was cast in the Warner Bros. film "G" Men, with James Cagney. Warner Bros., home of Cagney, Robinson and Muni, *The Public Enemy, Little Caesar, I Am a Fugitive*. But with the arrival of the Hays Office and the Motion Picture Production Code, which frowned upon the glorification of gangsters, the Brothers had to find different vehicles for their stars. Cagney would team up with his buddy Pat O'Brien in the first of eight screen teamings; Robinson would move more into character parts; Muni donned a beard and sideburns to portray the likes of Louis Pasteur and Emile Zola.

But the staple of Warner Bros. was crime films. Cagney, Robinson and Muni were the big three. What to do? The answer was to make Cagney a cop. But not just an ordinary cop. If Cagney was going to be on the side of Law and Order, let him be a top-rung copper, a G-Man.

The roots of the Federal Bureau of Investigation go back to the Theodore Roosevelt administration. For the next two-and-a-half decades, the Bureau underwent several name changes. In 1924, John Edgar Hoover became the director and, in 1935, the Bureau finally got the name it holds today. It was that year that the Warners decided to recognize the name with a film about the Bureau starring Cagney as an agent, using a novel by Gregory Rogers, *Public Enemy Number 1*. But Warner Bros. chose the title of "*G*" *Men*, a phrase given to F.B.I. Agents by George "Machine Gun" Kelly upon his arrest. Gregory Rogers, in reality, was Darryl F. Zanuck, who had left Warner Bros. to form his new 20th Century Pictures in 1934. The company would merge with Fox Film Corp. to form 20th Century-Fox in 1935, but the Rogers Zanuck script would remain at Burbank; and Rogers-Zanuck was the write-in candidate for an Academy Award for Best Original Story.

The story concerns attorney Brick Davis (Cagney), who was taken from the streets and a potential life of crime by a racketeer named McKay (William Harrigan). Davis' practice is struggling and a visit from his friend Eddie Buchanan (Regis Toomey), now an F.B.I. agent, prompts him to think about joining the Bureau. When Buchanan is murdered by the Brad Collins (Barton MacLane) Gang, Brick joins the Bureau. Saying goodbye to his girlfriend Jean Morgan (Ann Dvorak), he leaves for Washington. Upon arrival, Davis meets his instructors, Jeff McCord (Robert Armstrong) and Hugh Farrell (Lloyd), as well as McCord's sister Kay (Margaret Lindsay). The meeting with the McCords is like oil and water, but Brick takes an immediate liking to Farrell. When Farrell is murdered in a replication of the infamous Kansas City Massacre of 1933, Davis joins McCord in rounding up the F.B.I.'s ten most wanted. Along the way Collins murders McKay and Jean, kidnaps Kay, and gets his at the end. Cagney gets Kay and McCord gets a brother-in-law.

For this first on-screen appearance Lloyd registers well. Irene Thirer, in *The New York Post*, advised movie fans to "watch this lad."

Howard Barnes in *The New York Herald Tribune* called Nolan "excellent." Lloyd showed no signs of an actor making his maiden screen voyage. He looks the part of an F.B.I. agent and uses his physique well in a scene in the Bureau's gymnasium. If it were possible to look into the future, you would see his Hugh Farrell morphing into George Briggs, the character Lloyd played in both *The House on 92nd Street* and *The Street with No Name*. As for the film, it was an instant hit. And why not? Cagney was Cagney, but this time on the right side of the law; William Keighley's direction was crisp and fast-paced; and the supporting cast was typical Warner Bros. with Dvorak a particular standout. Her scenes with Cagney are emotional, yet sharp. It is a shame that her talents were seldom used to this advantage. One of her best scenes was the production number staged by Warner Bros.' resident choreographer Bobby Connolly. Miss Dvorak leads a chorus line in a dance number to Sammy Fain and Irving Kahal's "You Bother Me An Awful Lot." The number came close to not being filmed. Executive Producer Hal Wallis only wanted to have a soundtrack with Dvorak just singing. Wallis didn't want to spend the money for that much preparation. Connolly was allowed only an hour for rehearsal just prior to shooting. He made it work.

Jack Warner had a great relationship with Hoover, and the Director was a consultant on much of the film. He approved all casting. The film was given the Department of Justice Seal of Approval. Sources report that the film was banned in Chicago because of its violence. In 1949, Warner Bros. re-released the film to celebrate the twenty-fifth anniversary of Hoover's appointment, and added a new Prologue that featured David Brian and Douglas Kennedy.

The film's original release coincided with the trial of Adam Richetti, accused of being one of the Kansas City Station Plaza killers. Richetti's attorneys asked prospective jurors if they had seen "G" Men and if the picture created a new respect for federal agents. Those venire men who said they were influenced were excused. As a note, Richetti was found guilty and was executed in 1938.

Hoover would rule over the Bureau for a sum total of forty-eight years. His autonomy was so strong, he could not be replaced. He loved Hollywood because it would promote the F.B.I.'s credo: Fidelity, Bravery, Integrity. Both Jack Warner and Darryl Zanuck presented the F.B.I. in that light. Warners' contributions would include *The F.B.I. Story* in 1959, a Mervyn LeRoy production that starred James Stewart. While the film had some authentic moments, it was too much soap opera. The best episode was the final one with great on-location New York City shots. In 1965 Warner Bros produced a TV series called *The F.B.I.* It starred Efrem Zimbalist Jr., Stephen Brooks (later replaced by William Reynolds) and Phillip Abbott. The series was a major success, lasting nine seasons. In 2009, Zimbalist was honored with a plaque and a badge, making him an honorary F.B.I. Agent.

As for Zanuck's contribution, that would come some ten years later, and Lloyd would have a major part in it.

CHAPTER 6
Hero and Heavy, Cop and Crook

Lloyd's home studio, Paramount, finally used him themselves. Lloyd played the role of Chesty Burrage in the film *Stolen Harmony*, starring George Raft. It was a good role, but the movie was bad. It did serve to show producers that Lloyd could be a charming "good guy," though. Hal Erickson, in his *All Movie Guide,* wrote "… Nolan was, if not a star, certainly one of Hollywood's most versatile second-echelon leading men. As film historian William K. Everson has pointed out, the secret to Nolan's success was his integrity—the audience respected his characters."

The film's star, George Raft, whose reputation was that of a "bad boy," had an upbringing quite the opposite of Lloyd's. Born in the Hell's Kitchen section of New York City, Raft had a violent childhood, which eventually led him to a life of small-time crime and a relationship with several of Gotham's criminal types, who would aid him in getting into films. Raft was a smash hit in Howard Hawks' *Scarface*, stealing the film from its star, Paul Muni, with his ad-libbed coin flipping. His success led to a contract with Paramount, an incongruous choice as his on-screen and off-screen character was more suited to

Warner Bros. The Adolph Zukor-run Paramount specialized in sophisticated comedies, musicals, and the early Marx Brothers farces.
Cops-and-robbers films were not their forte and Raft's output at Paramount was not as career-advancing as it should have been.

Stolen Harmony is the story of vaudeville dancer Ray Ferraro
(Raft), who is about to be released from prison, having served time
for a minor crime. While incarcerated, he becomes an accomplished
saxophone player. He's hired by bandleader Jack Conrad (Ben Bernie), changes his name to Ray Angelo, and falls in love with singer
Jean Loring (Grace Bradley). Eventually, Ray's past catches up with
him and the film culminates with gang leader Chesty Burrage (Lloyd)
shooting Ray before getting gunned down himself. Ray recovers and
gets Jean at the end.

The casting was unusual. Bernie was a real-life bandleader and
songwriter who co-wrote "Sweet Georgia Brown." Bernie, who at the
time was having a mock feud with columnist Walter Winchell, a la
Jack Benny and Fred Allen, shows why he was a successful bandleader
and not an actor. Highlighting a Who's Who of Gangsters was William Cagney, brother of James. He played a member of Lloyd's Burrage gang. Lloyd would become friends with both Bill and Jim as the
years went on. But it was Lloyd who stole the film. *The New York Times*
review of the film singled Lloyd out as "being the only bright spot of
the picture." Raft came off as "saturnine as ever" and Miss Bradley
was "mildly helpful as his dancing partner." Grace Bradley soon after
would retire from films to marry William Boyd (Hopalong Cassidy),
a union that would last thirty-five years, until Hoppy's death in 1972.

Despite Raft's reputation, Lloyd got along with him famously. In
Stone Wallace's Raft biography, *George Raft, The Man Who Would Be*

Bogart, Lloyd noted that he'd heard all about how troublesome Raft could be on the set, but when he worked with him on *Stolen Harmony,* he couldn't recall any production difficulties. Lloyd and Raft would team up twice more in the next five years. Each time Lloyd would outshine Raft.

Lloyd's first released film, "*G"Men,* had its premiere on April 18, 1935, but didn't officially open until May 4. *Stolen Harmony* had its general release on April 19, 1935, a day after "*G" Men's* premiere.

When Lloyd's commitment to Paramount was fulfilled, he then signed on with Columbia Pictures.

Columbia Pictures began on Poverty Row and, through the shrewd decisions of brothers Jack and Harry Cohn and Joseph Brandt, they rose to the status of a major. But, unless you were a director named Frank Capra or there for a one-time deal, Howard Hawks (*Twentieth Century*), budgets were small and casts were not top drawer. When Columbia got a top star, it was usually as punishment, as were the cases of Clark Gable and Claudette Colbert, both exiled to Gower Street for a Capra production called *Night Bus.* Gable and Colbert both got the last laugh as the film, renamed *It Happened One Night,* won Oscars for both of them, as well as Capra for directing, Robert Riskin for best screenplay, and the film itself for best picture.

Lloyd would make six quick films for Columbia. *Atlantic Adventure* (1935) and *You May Be Next* (1936) were directed by Albert S. Rogell. In the former, Lloyd, second-billed to Columbia's glamour girl, Nancy Carroll, really was the star of the film playing a wise-guy reporter who chases his former fiancée (Carroll) aboard a ship and eventually captures a gang of thieves and killers. Also featured in the cast is former silent-film comedian Harry Langdon, who was a major

Atlantic Adventure, with Nancy Carroll

star at one time, relegated to comic relief in second-rate films. *Daily Variety* reported, "Lloyd Nolan was a bit far fetched as an ace reporter on a metropolitan daily but carries through to excellent results." In *You May Be Next*, Lloyd plays a radio engineer who winds up being arrested, kidnapped, redeemed, and finally married to Ann Sothern. Douglass Dumbrille played the villain.

Other Columbia ventures were *One Way Ticket* (1935), directed by Herbert Biberman, the first film in which Lloyd received top billing. Once again, he played the hero, once again he went to jail, once again he got the girl, this time Peggy Conklin. In *Counterfeit* (1936), Lloyd played the leader of a counterfeiting gang who is captured by undercover agent Chester Morris. Erle C. Kenton directed and B. P. Schulberg, former head of Paramount and father of author Budd Schulberg,

One Way Ticket, with Peggy Conklin

Devil's Squadron, with Richard Dix

produced. Schulberg also produced *Lady of Secrets* (1936), directed by Marion Gering, whose best days were behind him. This woman's weepie features Lloyd in a flashback as a lover to the star, Ruth Chatterton. Also in the cast were Lionel Atwill, Marian Marsh, and Otto Kruger. Lloyd got the best notices in a thankless part. Another Columbia production was *The Devil's Squadron* (1936), also directed by Erle C. Kenton. In this one, Lloyd plays a test pilot and friend to the star, Richard Dix. Dix has a past but is a hero at the end. Karen Morley is the female lead. Gordon Jones, later to be known as "Mike the Cop" on the Abbott and Costello TV show, led a large supporting cast.

Lloyd did have one high-end film at Columbia, and it was, once again, with George Raft. It was called *She Couldn't Take It* (1935). It had been B. P. Schulberg's first film at Columbia and was one of those screwball comedies in which Columbia excelled. Along with Raft, on loan-out from Paramount, Joan Bennett was the female lead, and Tay Garnett, a top-line director, was at the helm. The story finds bootlegger Spot Ricardi (Raft) sharing a jail cell with millionaire Daniel Van Dyke (Walter Connolly), who pled guilty to income tax evasion to get away from his greedy family. Van Dyke and Ricardi become friends and, when Van Dyke dies in prison, he appoints Ricardi executor of his estate. Part of his job is to keep Van Dyke's daughter Carol (Bennett) in check. Carol does not appreciate Ricardi (now Joe Ricard) controlling the purse strings, so she seeks out Ricardi's former partner Tex (Lloyd) to fake a kidnapping and split the ransom. Things go awry and Tex really kidnaps Carol. Ricardi comes to the rescue, shoots Tex, and rescues Carol. The film boasted a fine supporting cast. Besides Connolly, there was Billie Burke, Wallace Ford, Alan Mowbray, Frank Conroy, Franklin Pangborn, Donald Meek, and Tom Kennedy helping to move the proceedings along.

Raft, who had no experience in this genre, came off very well. *The New York Herald Tribune* said that Raft "had the most ingratiating characterization since the days he was playing minor villains," and *Liberty* magazine proclaimed that "Raft and Joan Bennett were excellent as the battling lovers," and went on to say that Raft "emerges with his best role since 'Scarface.'" It is a shame that Raft never had an opportunity to play this type of role until he was well past his prime. His two cameos in *Some Like It Hot* and *Ocean's Eleven* give testimony to Raft's flair for comedy. Lloyd received no special recognition as this type of role was becoming routine.

In between Columbia films was *Big Brown Eyes* (1936) for Paramount and a reunion with Joan Bennett, for her husband Walter Wanger. This time Miss Bennett is teamed with Cary Grant (a replacement for Fred MacMurray) and Walter Pidgeon. In this comedy-mystery Grant plays a cop, Dan Barr, who has had a fifteen-year relationship with manicurist Eve Fallon marked by love and fights. Lloyd plays a henchman involved with jewel thieves who accidentally kills a baby, and Pidgeon is the chief crook. Raoul Walsh gets a lot into seventy-seven minutes.

Lloyd got the best notices again. *Variety* said, "Exceptionally fine is the part of a killer crook as played by Lloyd Nolan."

There would be one more film for Lloyd before moving back to Paramount for a multi-year stretch. It was for 20th Century-Fox, where he was in support of Claire Trevor and Cesar Romero in *15 Maiden Lane* (1936), directed by the prolific Allan Dwan. Lloyd plays a cop who rescues Miss Trevor, who is an amateur undercover sleuth.

After working for three studios in two years and grinding out a succession of "A" and "B" films, Lloyd was ready to settle down at a professional home. And Paramount Pictures was ready for him.

Working in film was good in some ways, bad in others. Moviemaking did not have the rehearsal time that he was accustomed to on the stage, but that meant his delivery would be fresh and more spontaneous. It seemed, too, that people who formerly attended plays were now going to movies instead. It was a sign of the times and the stage was suffering.

Lloyd and Mell bought a small ranch of over 100 acres in the San Fernando Valley. Because Mell owned some horses, they had a track added so she could exercise them. They also made a mutually-advantageous deal with a ranch hand—he and his family could live on the

Early publicity shot of Lloyd

land for free and earn money by growing and selling both vegetables and their own livestock. The only stipulation was that they take good care of the ranch and Mell's horses. The man agreed and fulfilled his duties well.

Once Nolan's commitment to Columbia was over, Paramount signed him up again.

CHAPTER 7
The Paramount Years

Paramount Pictures' history goes back to 1912, when a New York nickelodeon operator named Adolph Zukor secured the rights to Sarah Bernhardt's four-reel film, *Queen Elizabeth*. It would be the first full-length drama shown in the United States. The amazing success of this event led to Zukor's forming The Famous Players Film Company. After a few successful New York productions, Zukor invested in a film-distribution company named Paramount Pictures. Four years later, when Famous Players merged with the Hollywood-based Jesse L. Lasky Company and the result was The Famous Players Lasky Corporation, it established the Paramount logo (reportedly modeled after Utah's Ben Lomond mountain).

Now considered the oldest of all film production companies, Paramount grew throughout the twenties. In 1927, the Paramount production *Wings* won the first Academy Award as Best Picture.

While MGM would claim that they "had more stars than were in the heavens," Paramount was no slouch when it came to talent. Gary Cooper, Fredric March, Carole Lombard, Bing Crosby, Marlene Dietrich, Cary Grant, Mae West, Jeanette MacDonald, Sylvia Sidney, Maurice Chevalier, W. C. Fields, and the Marx Brothers were among the performers under contract to Paramount. Directors like Cecil B. DeMille, Ernst Lubitsch, Josef von Sternberg, Henry Hathaway, and Leo McCarey were Paramount employees. Popeye the Sailor, Betty Boop and Koko the Clown came to life at the Marathon Street Studio where Max Fleischer toiled as a major force in cartoons.

Paramount's New York production presence helped them recruit talent from the stage. Paramount had noticed Lloyd's performance in *One Sunday Afternoon*. In early 1934, they signed him to a contract. As was often the case, studios would sign talent and never bother to use them, looking for the right property. Lloyd's case was no exception. He had appeared in one Paramount picture, *Stolen Harmony*, and had fared well. (Another was a Paramount release, *Big Brown Eyes*, but it was a Walter Wanger Production, made in-between his Columbia assignments.) On the strength of that and his performance in *"G" Men*, Lloyd was able to sign a contract with Columbia, building up his stock with a variety of portrayals. And Paramount, this time, took notice. Now noticing Lloyd's versatility as an actor, the company would be giving him steady work at Marathon Street.

His first assignment was *The Texas Rangers* (1936). It was a major project, produced, directed, and written by King Vidor. This would be Lloyd's western. The cast was first rate. Up-and-coming Fred MacMurray was the lead in a role originally written for Gary Cooper, Jean Parker, the female lead, Jack Oakie, Lloyd, Frank Shannon (Dr. Zarkov in the *Flash Gordon* serials), Charles Middleton (Ming in the *Flash Gordon* serials), and venerable western actor George "Gabby" Hayes headed a cast of over five hundred.

The plot has three happy-go-lucky outlaws, Jim Hawkins (MacMurray), Wahoo (Oakie) and Sam McGee (Lloyd), splitting up after escaping the law. Jim and Wahoo join the Texas Rangers, Sam becomes a cattle rustler. The trio meet up and they plan to use inside information gleaned from the rangers to plan some heists. On the way back to the outpost, Jim and Wahoo rescue David, a young survivor of an Indian raid. The daughter of the post commander (Parker) takes to rearing the boy and, in the meantime, falls in love with Jim. After proving himself a hero, Jim finds himself having to arrest Sam. Jim refuses. Wahoo goes out to arrest Sam, but is killed by his former partner, who now kidnaps David. Jim then goes after Sam, rescues David and shoots Sam when he refuses to surrender.

There were a couple of issues in the film that gave King Vidor concern. His screenplay walked a slippery slope with Sam's murder of Wahoo. Oakie's Wahoo was used for comedic balance, offsetting the seriousness of MacMurray's Jim and the villainy of Lloyd's Sam. A year earlier, Oakie had made *Call of the Wild* for Zanuck and his character died in the film. Audiences reacted negatively as this type of character seldom perished on screen (an exception was Jimmy Durante's character in 1932's *The Wet Parade*). Fox had to reshoot the scene with Oakie's character surviving. In addition, production was held up for several days due to a severe dust storm near Gallup. On the historic side was the fact that when Vidor filmed the train robbery, he was able to use the oldest-operating locomotive, "Montezuma #1."

The Texas Rangers was released to coincide with Texas' centennial. The timing was impeccable.

The uniqueness of the experience was new for Lloyd; this was his first time on location with the exteriors shot in Gallup, New Mexico, and Santa Fe, New Mexico. Once again, his notices were enthusiastic. *The New York Times* called his characterization "a pleasing sinister one." Lloyd was going up.

One of Lloyd's favorite roles of all time had been that of Sam "Polka Dot" McGee. MacMurray was always a pleasure to work with. Jack Oakie and Lloyd would good-naturedly compete with each other for the best camera angle in each screen. All three men enjoyed a good relationship when working on this project.

Paramount would remake *The Texas Rangers* in 1949, this time called *Streets of Laredo*, with William Holden, William Bendix and Macdonald Carey in the MacMurray, Oakie and Nolan roles. This version would be shot in Technicolor.

Lloyd was back as a gangster, this time in modern garb, in his next feature, *Interns Can't Take Money*, based on a Max Brand novel. Barbara Stanwyck, Joel McCrea and Lloyd, in a good-sized role, topped the list of players. This was the first film to feature the character of Dr. Jimmy Kildare (McCrea), who first treats Janet Haley (Stanwyck), who has fainted, and then a gangster Hanlon (Lloyd), who has been knifed. Janet, a widow of a bank robber who served time for harboring a fugitive, has a daughter who is kidnapped. She needs $1,000 to pay sleazebag Dan Innes (Stanley Ridges) for information about the child. Hanlon gratefully gives Kildare the thousand, which Janet tries to steal. The doctor has to return the money as interns are not allowed to accept payment. Hanlon hears about Janet's plight and rounds up his gang to "convince" Innes to talk. Innes is shot, though, and Kildare has to perform an experimental liver operation to save his life. Innes talks, the daughter is rescued, and the curtain falls.

While McCrea played Dr. Jimmy Kildare, Paramount had no plans to continue the character. The rights to the rest of Brand's work would go to MGM, where they made a successful series out of Kildare's dramas at Blair General Hospital, starring Lew Ayres as Kildare and Lionel Bar-

rymore as Dr. Gillespie. (In *Interns*, the hospital was known as Mount-
view General Hospital in New York. In addition, there was no kindly Dr.
Gillespie.) When Ayres left the series, Barrymore continued with the
series in a quartet of films, which featured young MGM players like Van
Johnson, Philip Dorn and Donna Reed. In the sixties MGM television
resurrected the characters to capitalize on the doctor show craze. Richard Chamberlain was Kildare, Raymond Massey was Gillespie.

In filming *Interns Can't Take Money*, Paramount utilized the ser
vices of Dr. John J. Toma, the chief resident of Hollywood Hospital.
Also in the cast were ten interns from the same hospital. There is no
knowledge if any of them took money for their work.

Robert Florey would direct Lloyd's next film. It is a shame that his
contributions to films were never appreciated, but his French expression-
ist roots show up in every one of his numerous efforts. Florey learned his
craft in his native France, and began directing when he got to the US in the
twenties. He would direct films until 1950, with his swan song being Errol
Flynn's *The Adventures of Captain Fabian* for Republic. But his career wasn't
over. He slid into television and directed episodes of *The Twilight Zone*,
Perry Mason, *The Alfred Hitchcock Show* and *The Loretta Young Show* (where
he received an Emmy nomination), among others.

For Paramount, Florey directed the Marx Brothers' first film, *The
Cocoanuts*. He moved to Warner Bros. for a few years, coming back to
Paramount in 1936, where he worked on many of their programmers.
In *King of Gamblers* (1937), he had Akim Tamiroff, along with Claire
Trevor and Lloyd. He also had Helen Burgess, Harvey Stephens, Porter
Hall and Larry Crabbe (a.k.a. "Buster"), incongruously cast as a heavy.

According to Rose Pelswick, writing in the *New York Journal American* in 1937, Lloyd's casting in this film was a direct result of public

Lloyd, Akim Tamiroff, and Claire Trevor in *King of Gamblers*

opinion. After *The Texas Rangers*, moviegoers had written letters to Paramount complaining about Lloyd's casting. Studio executives and writers didn't care; they cast Lloyd as a heavy in *Interns Can't Take Money*, but this time they gave him a soft side. It mattered not. By the time that film was in release, the letters of protest had assumed such proportions that studio authorities decided that something had to be done.

What was done was assigning Lloyd the role of a hero, Jimmy Adams, a reporter who, along with a nightclub singer Dixie Moore (Claire Trevor), takes down gangster Steve Kalkas (Tamiroff). In the end they succeed. Both *The Hollywood Reporter* and *The Daily Variety* praised Lloyd's work. *The Reporter* noted that Lloyd "exhibited none of the heroics of the traditional movie reporter and wins liking as a natural and resourceful human being." *Variety* said that "Lloyd Nolan, Akim Tamiroff and Claire Trevor vie for acting honors."

Lloyd was a bad guy again in *Exclusive*, this time racketeer Charlie Gilette, who buys a newspaper looking to get revenge on the Better Government Committee members who had unsuccessfully tried to put him in jail for his crimes. He is opposed by an honest newspaper editor Ralph Houston (Fred MacMurray). Frances Farmer was the female lead; Charles Ruggles, Ralph Morgan, and Horace McMahon were also in the Alexander Hall-directed film. Again, Lloyd stood out in his notices. *The Hollywood Reporter* said, "Lloyd Nolan's master crook is a portrait of quietly sinister power" and *The Daily Variety* noted that "Lloyd Nolan delivers his excellent standard performance in urbane villainy." It was while making *Exclusive* Lloyd met the director's girlfriend, Lucille Ball. They would become great friends.

Lloyd's next role would be his first in Technicolor, *Ebb Tide*. The South Sea tale starred Ray Milland, Frances Farmer and Oscar Homolka, with Lloyd and Barry Fitzgerald having the biggest supporting parts. Lloyd played a character named Attwater, the self-proclaimed ruler of an island that the protagonists land on in search of food. Henry Hathaway was to direct, but he was tied up with *Souls At Sea*, so the reigns of this third telling of Robert Louis Stevenson's tale were given to James Hogan, one of Paramount's "B" directors. The best notices were given to the Technicolor photography, as well as Lloyd's (*Variety* called him "excellent") and Fitzgerald's acting.

Then it was back to the west for Lloyd, in another big-budget film, *Wells Fargo*, the semi-fictional story of the famous western stage line. Originally, Paramount planned to have Fred MacMurray, Frances Farmer and Randolph Scott star, but came upon the unique idea of

Wells Fargo

having real-life husband-and-wife team Joel McCrea and Frances Dee play the leads with Bob Burns and Lloyd in support. This film held the promise of a Cecil B DeMille epic, but after a rousing start director Frank Lloyd, himself an "A" list helmsman having directed Oscar winners *Cavalcade* in 1933 and *Mutiny on the Bounty* two years later, allowed the film to settle into a soap opera with segments of spectacular action. Lloyd appeared in only one part of this episodic film, and he was at his most despicable playing Del Slade who ambushes McCrea's Ramsay McKay. McCrea and Miss Dee gave good performances in their first film together since their 1933 marriage. (The couple had met while appearing together in RKO's *The Silver Cord* and made *One Man's Journey* for the same studio. They would appear one more time over a decade later, in the underrated *Four Faces West*.)

Dangerous to Know with Roscoe Karns, Anthony Quinn, and Harvey Stephens

Next up at Paramount was *Dangerous to Know*, based on the 1930 Broadway play *On the Spot*, written by Edgar Wallace, reportedly in four days, and inspired by the career of Al Capone. It reunited Lloyd, Akim Tamiroff and Robert Florey with Anna May Wong reprising her stage role. Gail Patrick and Anthony Quinn also had major parts in the proceedings.

Tamiroff plays Stephen Recka, a gangster with a Napoleonic complex who not only wants to take over a city but marry socialite Margaret Van Kasse (Gail Patrick). A city inspector, Brandon (Lloyd), is convinced that Recka has committed eight murders but does not have any evidence to back up his suspicions. Recka sends his henchman Nicolai "Nicky" Kusnoff (Anthony Quinn) off to get information on Margaret's fiancé Philip Easton (Harvey Stephens). Recka's mistress, Lan Ying (Anna May Wong), cautions Recka that trying to reach into society is beyond his grasp. Recka has Philip framed, Margaret offers to marry Recka if she frees Philip, Lan Ying eventually commits suicide, Recka is arrested for the murder of Lan Ying, and Margaret and Philip head off happily.

The Daily Variety said, "Lloyd picks up the tempo of the film in all of his scenes," and *The Hollywood Reporter* claimed that Lloyd was "more than adequate."

Lloyd was working in B movies and was usually cast as either a gangster or a policeman. He seemed to some to have many of the same qualities as James Cagney, so received similar roles.

The final film of Lloyd's Paramount contract was *Every Day's a Holiday*, a comedy starring Mae West. In spite of Mae's superstar status and the fact that she wrote this comedy, mustachioed Lloyd held his own. He plays the corrupt police inspector John Quade who decides to run for mayor. Captain McCarey (played by Edmund Lowe), an honest cop who disgusts Quade, is also running for that office. They both have a romantic interest in Peaches O'Day (Mae West's character), a con artist who has dozens of warrants out for her arrest. Peaches, who was posing as a performer named Mademoiselle Fifi, rebuffs Quade; so he threatens to close down the theater. Peaches goes to visit him to convince him to leave it open, but still artfully dodges his kisses. When it looks like McCarey has more support for mayor than he does, evil Quade has him kidnapped. Of course, the good guy (McCarey) saves the day and provides a happy ending. Even Louis Armstrong made a cameo appearance as he led the marching band. It was Lloyd's idea for the safe's door to open whenever Mae West patted it. She didn't see the humor in this, but the audience did. *The*

Lloyd with Mae West in *Every Day's a Holiday*

Hollywood Reporter claimed that "although Lloyd Nolan was miscast, he was too good an actor not to make something of the part." Some moviegoers felt that Lloyd was the best part of the movie; Mae West fans disagreed. Both were superb.

Lloyd would do more films for Paramount in the future, but not contracted. He refused to sign a new contract with them. It wasn't that he disliked working there. In fact, Paramount provided a much less tense environment than MGM had, but Lloyd just wanted his freedom.

Paramount was developing its own Murder's Row, just as Warner Bros. had done with many of their contract players like Barton MacLane, Joseph Downing, Edward Pawley, Russell Hopton, and Noel Madison. Paramount answered with the likes of Anthony Quinn, Larry Crabbe, Akim Tamiroff, J. Carrol Naish, and Horace McMahon. Lloyd could consider himself a part of this crew as well.

In his first film as a freelancer, Lloyd went back to a good old Paramount cops-and-robbers programmer, *Tip-Off Girls*.

Paramount was another studio that would pander to J. Edgar Hoover's request that Hollywood make films portraying his agents as heroes as Warner Bros. did with *"G" Men*. Among others in Paramount's F.B.I. series were *Persons in Hiding, Illegal Traffic, Undercover Doctor* and *Queen of the Mob*. In *Tip-Off Girls*, Lloyd plays an F.B.I. agent, Bob Anders. Anders and his partner Tom Benson (Roscoe Karnes) attempt to break up a truck-hijacking gang run by Red Deegan (Larry Crabbe), who works for racketeer Joseph Valkus (J. Carrol Naish). The gang's MO involves Red's girl Rena (Evelyn Brent) posing as a motorist in distress, thus distracting the driver. While working for Red, Bob meets Valkus' secretary Marjorie (Mary Carlisle), who does not realize that Valkus is a crime boss. At the end

Lloyd and Mary Carlisle in *Tip-Off Girls*

the end of the Louis King-directed sixty-one-minute quickie, Bob
and Tom break the gang and Bob gets Marjorie.

Much of the same personnel were involved with *Hunted Men*
(1938). Once again, Lloyd was the lead. Once again, Mary Carlisle got
top billing with Lloyd second. The usual suspects were there: J. Carrol
Naish, Larry Crabbe, Anthony Quinn, and Louis King directed. The
difference in this one was that Lloyd played Joe Albany, a racketeer
who kills his dishonest partner (Crabbe). He finds refuge with a family
and gets redeemed by the daughter (Carlisle) and young son (Delmar
Watson). Lynne Overman and Dorothy Peterson play the parents, and
Regis Toomey was also in the cast as a young cop. *The Hollywood Reporter*, in its review, praised Lloyd in the headline and gave him the

most comprehensive review to date: "In Lloyd Nolan as the gangster, director Louis King has the sympathetic heavy needed to give the considerable subtlety of shading to the role. Nolan, in fact, portrays admirably the development of a man from a selfish and egotistical killer to being capable of the ultimate sacrifice for others."

Next came *Prison Farm* (1938). The only difference between this and the previous two was that Shirley Ross played the female lead and was top-billed over Lloyd. Louis King again directed, J. Carrol Naish was again in support, as was John Howard, Marjorie Main and Porter Hall. Lloyd plays Larry Harrison, a killer on the lam who meets waitress Jean Forrest and convinces her to run away with him to Canada. They are both arrested and sent to Prison Farms. Jean can't take the life there; eventually, she is taken under the wing of the prison doctor (John Howard). Naish plays a crooked prison guard who kills Larry and is exposed at the end.

Both Ralph Murphy and then Herbert Biberman were scheduled to direct this film, but shooting had to be postponed till October 1937 to coincide with the cotton-picking season.

King of Alcatraz was another of those programmers that Robert Florey made for Paramount. This time Gail Patrick received top billing but the real heroes in the film were Lloyd and a young actor, Robert Preston, making his first film. Lloyd and Preston are two battling sailor buddies (Ray and Bob) who are assigned to the *S.S. Escobar* captained by Captain Glennon (Harry Carey). They are joined on board by the ship's nurse, Dale Borden (Gail Patrick), a former fiancée of Ray, and Bonnie Larkin (Virginia Dabney), along with her grandmother, Mrs. Farnsworth, who in reality is escaped convict Steve Murkil (J. Carrol Naish). Murkill takes over the ship, Ray and

Bob try to radio for help, Ray gets shot, and after the crew overpowers Murkil, Dale performs an operation by wireless instruction, saving Ray's life and marrying him at the end.

Another fine supporting cast graced this fifty-eight-minute action-packed adventure.   Anthony Quinn, Porter Hall, Richard Denning, Konstantin Shayne, Tom Tyler and Monte Blue were among those that had parts. Another member of the cast was Richard Stanley, who played First Mate Rogers. This was Stanley's first released film using that name. (His first actual film with that name was *Men with Wings*, shot prior but released later.) Earlier, in films like *The Great Ziegfeld*, he used the name Stanley Morner. After his Paramount days ended, he moved to Warner Bros., where he changed his name again … to Dennis Morgan.

Gladys Swarthout was not known as an actress, but as a major operatic singer. Opera films and stars made money for the studios in the mid-thirties. MGM had the duo of Jeanette MacDonald and Nelson Eddy, RKO had Lily Pons, and Columbia had Grace Moore. The genre was so popular that MGM tailored an opera-themed film for their first Marx Brothers film, *A Night at the Opera,* which was a major smash hit and gave rebirth to the Marxes. Paramount's answer to the opera film was Gladys Swarthout. Her resume was attractive, her mezzo voice melodic. Her signature role of "Carmen" was hailed by critics all over the world. Unfortunately, despite her reputation, the four operatic films she made between 1936 and 1938 were all failures. As is the case in Hollywood, when a big money talent can't justify her salary, it's best to cut your losses. Ms. Swarthout would not be allowed a big budget for her last Paramount feature. Instead, she would be top-billed in *Ambush* (1939), a programmer which co-starred Lloyd.

The good guy-bad guy pendulum this time pointed to a good-guy role for Lloyd. Here he plays Tony Andrews, a truck driver lured into

Candid of Jane Wyatt and unidentified woman with Lloyd

the service of a gang headed by a Mr. Gibbs (Ernest Truex) after they've committed a daring robbery. Second in command is Randall (Broderick Crawford), and another member of the gang is a wimpy Charlie Hartman (William Henry). Charlie's sister Jane (Ms. Swarthout) happens to be a witness to the gang's crime, and she is abducted, too. At the end Tony helps capture the crooks and Ms. Swarthout as well.

Despite her only non-singing role, *Daily Variety* said the film presented the singer-actress in a better characterization, and also complimented Lloyd for "a sure performance." *The Hollywood Reporter* singled out both Lloyd and Broderick Crawford for standing out "with particular emphasis." Despite the good notice, this was the final film for Gladys Swarthout.

Up until now, Lloyd had appeared in almost every genre, playing every type of character. The three categories missing from his resume were historical (studio heads couldn't picture him playing a knight), war (which would shortly become a signature component of his portfolio) and the musical. Melodies, harmonies, and Lloyd would mix in his next film, *St. Louis Blues*, a film which starred Paramount's resident "sarong" girl, Dorothy Lamour, who plays Norma Malone, an actress known on Broadway as "Aloma," a role she portrays on the stage. Norma is tired of this role so she runs away and, incognito, takes refuge on a Mississippi riverboat, where she meets the ship's impresario, Dave Gurney (Lloyd). Unaware of who she really is, Dave gives her a job but not a part in the boat's show, thinking she's an amateur. The cast and crew of the boat go through all sorts of adventures, culminated by Norma beautifully singing a song to a judge who wants to throw them all in jail. Dave, now in love with Norma, realizes he has a star and starts to showcase her. Word gets back to Broadway and her manager (Jerome Cowan) tries to grant an injunction preventing her from appearing in Dave's revue. Norma finds a loophole in her contract, and stays with the boat and Dave.

In a portent of things to come, George Raft turned down the role of Dave, leaving it for Lloyd who made the most of playing second fiddle to Dorothy Lamour. Lloyd would be far more effective a few years later in similar-themed film, *Blues in the Night*. The score, with the title tune by W.C. Handy and several by Frank Loesser, was okay if not memorable.

St. Louis Blues was directed by Raoul Walsh, finishing out his contract at Paramount. He would move on to Warner Bros., where he would direct some of his most famous films, including Humphrey Bogart's *High Sierra* (another Raft reject), Errol Flynn's *They Died With Their Boots On*, and James Cagney's *White Heat*.

St. Louis Blues with Dorothy Lamour

After the unusual casting that *St Louis Blues* offered, it was back again to cops and robbers for the third and final Louis King programmer, this one *Undercover Doctor*. In an earlier collaboration, Lloyd played a character named Bob Anders. This time he plays the same character, an F.B.I. agent. The title is misleading as the Doctor is played by J. Carrol Naish and he's not undercover. He's a medic for a bunch of crooks led by Broderick Crawford. The female leads are Janice Logan and Heather Angel. The end was as predictable as was the film.

There would be one more Paramount film before Lloyd would leave Marathon Street for greener pastures. It was *The Magnificent Fraud*, again reuniting Lloyd with Akim Tamiroff and director Robert Florey. Lloyd is Sam Barr, the right-hand assistant to the president of a small South American country (Tamiroff). The country is about to finalize a ten-million-dollar loan from the United States when the president is killed in an explosion. Barr calls upon an actor, Jules La Croix, to impersonate the dead president. However, another faction is looking to take over the country. By the end, the fraudulent leader is killed, the good faction led by Dr. Virgo (George Zucco) takes over the country, and Sam gets the girl (Patricia Morison, who would later become the original Lili Vanessi in the stage production of *Kiss Me, Kate*).

Once again Lloyd was the beneficiary of a George Raft reject and Lloyd was grateful for the job. He gave it his all and it showed. While reviewers praised Tamiroff in the showier part, Lloyd got his share of notices. *The Daily Variety* said, "Tamiroff carries his masquerade off effectively and Nolan gives good accounts of his talents as the arrogant and amative slicker from Chicago who is put on the defensive by the love he has provoked in the decorative Miss Morison." *The Hollywood Reporter* said, "Akim Tamiroff has the key role and he enacts it with consummate skill. Yet it barely overshadows the portrayal of Lloyd Nolan as the young Chicagoan who has grown to become the power behind the executive chair."

The story was based on an original novel by Charles G. Booth, *Caviar for His Excellency*. Booth would become involved with Lloyd in one of his most famous films a few years later, writing the original story for *The House on 92nd Street*. The story would also be the basis for the 1988 Paul Mazursky film, *Moon Over Parador*, with Richard Dreyfuss in the Tamiroff role and Raul Julia as Lloyd's character.

Besides Raft, others included in the original cast were Isa Miranda, slated for the part played by Patricia Morison, and smaller roles were assigned to Gene Lockhart and Anthony Quinn, who were replaced by Ernest Cossart and Abner Biberman. Those that did support Lloyd and Tamiroff in this venture were Ralph Forbes, Mary Boland and the underappreciated Steffi Duna (who shortly would give up her career to become the wife of actor Dennis O'Keefe, one of screendom's strongest marriages). Another member of the cast was actress Virginia Dabney. After the completion of this film, Miss Dabney became Mrs. Robert Florey. She would become very significant in Lloyd's life many years later.

Although Lloyd was contractually divorced from Paramount, he was offered an additional part by them. It was to be in a Cecil B DeMille film, *North West Mounted Police,* which would star Gary Cooper, Madeline Carroll, Preston Foster, Robert Preston, and Paulette Goddard. Lloyd was to play the main villain, Jacques Corbeau, but George Bancroft played the part instead.

Around this time, there was one story that has become very famous involving Lloyd and another western. Director John Ford was casting a new project and looking for a young veteran actor to play the protagonist, second billed to Claire Trevor. He called in a young actor he knew who had been working in "B" westerns and had done some small work for him before. He asked the young actor to read the script. The actor did so and Ford asked him who he thought should play the cowboy. The actor replied, "I think it will be a good part for Lloyd Nolan." Ford then laughed and told the actor, "It's not for Nolan, it's for you." The actor was hired and all worked out well as John Wayne would become a major star after playing the role of "The Ringo Kid" in the all-time classic *Stagecoach.*

Back at the ranch, Lloyd was enjoying life with Mell and their dogs.

"You *are* going to share, aren't you?"

CHAPTER 8

Welcome to Fox, But You Don't Have a Reserved Parking Space Yet

As the decade began, good things started to happen. Lloyd was free-lancing and would get plenty of work, much at a new home, 20th Century-Fox. Mell was now expecting a baby, so the couple felt it was time to buy a more conventional house. They found a beautiful one. It was an English Tudor-style home at 239 North Bristol Avenue, which was in the Brentwood section. Built in 1925, its price was now $13,000. This was to be not only the family home for the rest of their lives, but it was also a very good investment. About thirty years later, it would be re-appraised at around $250,000.

The house had some features that they did not need; so they had the balconies, fountain, and arches removed, replacing them with ceiling-high bookcases and a bar-enhanced lanai. Inside was Queen Ann and Victorian furniture, antique and otherwise, around an Oriental carpet. The home was beautiful, but comfortable and lived-in.

Don Lightfoot recalls:

They bought their house in Brentwood when they were expecting Melinda. That became, as Mell always stated, their ancestral home. It was a beautiful home with four bedrooms, servant quarters, basement with movie theater, and six bathrooms in the main house. A guest house was built above the three-car garage and a pool house with two changing rooms on the back of the garage. All total, they had six sleeping quarters and nine bathrooms. Mell once described the property as the perfect place if you had diarrhea. Later, a shop was added next to the changing rooms where Lloyd kept various tools for maintenance of the house and cars. He was perhaps one of the most unable persons I have ever met when it came to tools and maintenance of anything. Over the eleven years I knew Lloyd his tools never lost their new look and most probably never left their assigned place on the peg-board-lined walls of his shop.

Lloyd and Mell became proud parents of a precious baby girl on November 2, 1940. They would name her Melinda Joyce Nolan.

Now that he had a family to support, Lloyd more than ever needed the work. Considering the variety of the work Lloyd did for Paramount, Fox wasn't sure how to use him. His first effort was *The Man Who Wouldn't Talk,* a lower-case entry the *New York Times* called "an excellent little program picture—a picture, that is, ideally suited for the minor half of a double bill." Six writers combined on the film, including Robert Ellis and Helen Logan, who were respon-

An aerial view of the Nolan estate. (From the collection of Nolan Lightfoot)

sible for many of the Charlie Chan gems put out by Fox. Lloyd, in a role originally considered for Richard Barthelmess and then Humphrey Bogart, plays Joe Monday, who has confessed to the murder of businessman Frederick Keller (Onslow Stevens). But Joe has a secret and won't testify on his behalf. Seventy minutes later we find out why. Jean Rogers co-stars with Lloyd, who got some of the best notices of his career. *The Hollywood Reporter* said, "Nolan is Brilliant as the confessed killer, playing the role with an admirable and extremely effective restraint." *Daily Variety* was even more enthusiastic: "Lloyd Nolan is superb in the role of the murderer. His performance in the role of the martyr has a fatalistic punch of conviction which invests it with compassionate interest throughout."

The film was an adaptation of a one-act play, *The Valiant,* co-written by actor Robert Middlemass. It would be made by Fox in 1929 with Paul Muni starring in the role that Lloyd played. It would also be produced on early television in 1939 with Bert Lytell, who played the part on the stage, starring. Muni would do the part again in a television event in 1948. Lloyd's version of the story was the only one that had a happy ending, where the lead character is not executed for murder.

Lloyd would be reunited with George Raft and Joan Bennett again in 1940's *The House Across The Bay.* Producer Walter Wanger and Ms. Bennett were married and, as one would expect, Joan got the best of the photography, including twenty-six costume changes, playing Brenda Bentley, a nightclub singer who marries nightclub owner Steve Larwitt (Raft), who has his hands in several illegal operations. When a rival gang tries to kill Larwitt, Brenda turns him in to the feds on an income tax charge, thinking her hubby would be sent up for only a year, thus keeping the killers away from him. Instead, due to

The Man Who Wouldn't Talk with Richard Clarke and Jean Rogers

the corked efforts of Larwit's lawyer, Slant Kilma (Lloyd), Steve gets ten years in Alcatraz. Brenda takes a house on the other side of San Francisco Bay with a view of the rock to comfort her. Meanwhile, all Steve wants to do is to get out and find out who turned him in so he can even the books. Brenda meets aircraft builder Tim Nolan (Walter Pidgeon), who falls in love with her. While Tim and Joan lunch one day they encounter Slant, who tells her that Steve is broke. He also professes his love for her, but Brenda rejects him. Slant tells Steve that it was Brenda who turned him in; Steve escapes from Alcatraz, and looks to kill Brenda, finding her with Tim. They manage to convince Steve that Slant is the real traitor and that Brenda loves Tim. Steve finds Slant, kills him and tries to swim back to Alcatraz, but the guards' bullets get him before he reaches the Rock.

Warner Bros. originally had the rights to this story and planned to use it as a vehicle for James Cagney and Marlene Dietrich, but they passed on the project. It is interesting to think what they would have done with this. The Archie Mayo direction, while good, is missing that Warners' pace. At times the film becomes a soap opera, and the script, which has Raft escaping from Alcatraz, then going back, is a little hard to fathom. The production seems to move better when Raft is in the film. As for Lloyd, this is one of his most brilliant interpretations. He is the epitome of villainy, yet Lloyd so underplays the part of Slant, his evil sneaks up on you. It is arguably Lloyd's best bad-guy performance. *Daily Variety* reported, "Walter Pidgeon, Lloyd Nolan and Gladys George share honors."

Raft managed to make some off-screen news when Elizabeth Copeland reported in a 1940 article that Raft arrived at the studio with the Hollywood police on his tail. As the officers approached, Raft said, "I didn't think I was doing over forty." The policeman sheepishly replied that they thought he was an escaped convict driving a stolen car. Raft had been running late and drove to the studio in his prison costume.

Another visitor to the set was a famous director. He had just completed working on a film for Wanger and stopped by one day to say hello. As a favor to Wanger, he agreed to direct a scene in an airplane scene between two of the leading players. And that's how Joan Bennett and Walter Pidgeon came to be directed for a scene by the great Alfred Hitchcock.

Lloyd was a more conventional villain in his next Fox film, *Johnny Apollo*. Tyrone Power, Dorothy Lamour and Edward Arnold star in the story of a Bob Cain (Power), who comes from a wealthy background. When his father, Bob Sr. (Arnold), is found guilty of em-

L-R Marc Lawrence, Lloyd, Tyrone Power, Edward Arnold in *Johnny Apollo*

bezzlement, he is sent to prison and all of Bob's friends turn his back
on him. Unable to get a job or find legal methods to get his father
a parole, he meets up with gangster Mickey Dwyer (Lloyd) and his
girlfriend "Lucky" (Ms. Lamour). Bob, Jr. joins Dwyer's gang and
changes his name to Johnny Apollo. He is befriended by Lucky and
Dwyer's drunken lawyer, "Judge" Brennan (Charley Grapewin).
Johnny rises in Dwyer's organization and becomes the number-two
man. Dwyer kills Brennan when he finds out that Brennan is going

to turn him in exchange for amnesty for Apollo. Johnny, not realizing the deal, testifies in behalf of Mickey and both are sent to jail where father and son are reunited. After a failed escape, Mickey is killed, father and son mend their fences and Johnny marries Lucky.

For a studio that did not specialize in this type of genre, Fox did a slick job on this one, showcasing Power in something other than fluffy roles, supporting the likes of Loretta Young and Alice Faye. Henry Hathaway's direction is sure and not flashy. Dorothy has a few good numbers, and the supporting cast, which included Lionel Atwill, Marc Lawrence and Jonathan Hale, is first rate, with Lloyd once again standing out in a role he had perfected over the years.

Next came *Gangs of Chicago*. One would think that, with a cast that included Lloyd, Barton MacLane, Lola Lane, Horace McMahon and Addison Richards, this would come from Warner Bros. or Paramount. But this one came out of lower-level Republic, the first time Lloyd would work at a non-major studio. Originally, Samuel Fuller, who had written *Gangs of New York* a couple of years earlier for the same studio, was approached to write a screenplay; but if he ever contributed anything, it could not be confirmed.

Lloyd plays Matty Burns, the son of a gangster who was gunned down by the police. Matty goes to law school to learn how to use the law to help the mob. He is helped by a society gangster (Barton MacLane). He also forms a relationship with an honest family. Realizing the error of his ways, Matty sees he has to help break up the gang. He gets shot in the process, but the gang is broken up. Once he recovers, he knows he will go to jail.

Lloyd, as the star, got the best notices. *The Hollywood Reporter* said Lloyd Nolan is "fine as usual." *Daily Variety* reported, "Nolan executes his role capably for a standout performance."

Barton MacLane, Lloyd, Charles Halton, and Horace McMahon in *Gangs of Chicago*

Two significant members of the crew were borrowed from Universal Pictures. One was director Arthur Lubin, who would go on to do some Abbott and Costello films, and Elwood Bredel, who later shot some brilliant *film noirs*, including Mark Hellinger's *The Killers*.

It was back to Fox and another venture with Joan Bennett, their fourth together, *The Man I Married*. Lloyd's role was definitely a notch down from his previous Fox assignments. The reason for this was that Lloyd was a quick replacement for contract player Richard Greene, who was bedridden for two weeks with the flu. After scoring a major success as an American drawn into the German American Bund and becoming a full-fledged Nazi supporter in Warner Bros.' *Confessions of a Nazi Spy*, Francis Lederer was offered a similar type of role in this project when George Sanders, originally given the part, was unable to meet production date due to the fact that his current film, *Foreign Correspondent,* had gone over schedule. Lederer plays Eric Hoffman, a natural-born German living in the United States in 1938 with his wife Carol (Bennett), a magazine art critic, and son Ricky. Eric is asked to go back to Germany to help his father run the family business, and Carol sees this as an opportunity to take an extended family vacation. While in Germany, Eric begins to believe in the Nazi movement, which draws him away from his wife. When Eric decides to permanently relocate to Germany, he and Carol decide to divorce. Carol wants to return to the U.S., but Eric insists his son stay in Germany. With the help of a newspaperman, Ken Delane (Lloyd), Carol tries to smuggle Ricky out of Germany. Eric stops the escape. After a surprise revelation, Eric is disgraced. Carol and Ricky leave Germany for America, with Ken staying to cover the war.

Even though Lloyd had very little to do except utter a number of good satirical lines, his contribution was praised in *The Hollywood Reporter,* who wrote that "The American Newsman was played to a solid hit by Lloyd Nolan."

Lederer really came off well and Ms. Bennett was very good as well. The film also boasted a great scene-stealing performance by Otto Kruger in a change-of-pace sympathetic role. Anna Sten, Maria Ouspenskaya, and Ludwig Stossel were effective as well.

In a way Joan Bennett was connected with Lloyd's next film, *Pier 13.* It was a remake of a 1932 film, *Me and My Gal,* which starred Spencer Tracy and Ms. Bennett. Here, the leads are taken by Lloyd and Lynn Bari. Lloyd plays a cop; Ms Bari plays his girl. Also around are Joan Valerie and Douglas Fowley, who plays the baddie. It all cul-

Lloyd and Lynn Bari in *Pier 13*

minates in sixty-four minutes with a happy ending. It would be the first film that Lloyd would make under the directorial reins of Eugene Forde, who would become a favorite of Lloyd's.

Another of his favorites was co-star Lynn Bari. The feeling was mutual. Lloyd was one of Bari's favorite leading men because he treated her with respect and admiration, according to Colin Briggs, in his article about her in the December, 2009, issue of *Classic Images* magazine. "Lynn thought *very* highly of Lloyd and *always* enjoyed working with him," says her biographer, Jeff Gordon. "In order to make him 'look good,' she often took off her heels and went before the cameras in bedroom slippers—so she wouldn't photograph taller than he." The chemistry between Lynn and Lloyd was a boon to the

With Virginia Grey and Lew Ayres in *The Golden Fleecing*

box office with *Pier 13* (Lynn's favorite), so they were cast together in one Michael Shayne film, *Sleepers West,* and two other pictures, *Charter Pilot* and *Captain Eddie.* Lynn was also in Lloyd's *Fifteen Maiden Lane,* but it was as an extra in the crowd. "I was always delighted when I was going to be doing a film with him. He was a helluva actor," Lynn is quoted as saying in her biography, *Foxy Lady,* by Jeff Gordon. "We used to get loaded with the crew at wrap-up parties and tell stories. We always had a barrel of fun."

A barrel of fun was anticipated from Lloyd's next film, his first for the Tiffany of studios, MGM. It was called *The Golden Fleecing,* and it was directed Leslie Fenton, who was making the transition from actor to director. Fenton is best remembered for his role of "Nails Nathan" in *The Public Enemy*. This was Fenton's fourth full-length film, and it would be a comedy along the lines of the 1936 classic *Three Men on a Horse*. Lew Ayres, in a role intended for James Stewart, is Henry Twinkle, a milquetoast insurance salesman who sells an insurance policy to Gus Fender (Lloyd), not knowing he is a racketeer with a price on his head, dead or alive. Twinkle now has to make sure he doesn't get bumped off. After Gus is arrested in a small town on a minor charge, Twinkle is convinced to claim he turned him in so he can claim a reward to bail Gus out. Twinkle continues to mess things up for Gus, finally becoming a wealthy man. Gus has a chance to get out of the clink, but commits his own blunder and stays in jail.

This was another one of those roles that Lloyd could play in his sleep, and despite a great supporting MGM cast that included Rita Johnson, Virginia Grey, Leon Errol, Nat Pendleton, and the serial world's Dick Tracy, Ralph Byrd, the film definitely belonged on the bottom half of a double bill.

While Lloyd had been freelancing for several years, Twentieth Century-Fox finally came through with a contract. Lloyd would work for other studios during the forties, but his output at Fox would be his best and would contain some memorable performances.

One of those would not be his first contract assignment. *Charter Pilot* would reunite him with Lynn Bari in another programmer directed by Eugene Forde. Lloyd plays King Morgan the title player, Lynn Bari plays his girlfriend Marge Duncan, who writes about his daring deeds for a radio station. They meet up with a number of bad types before finally getting married at the end. One thing that Fox was

With Lynn Bari in *Charter Pilot* (Courtesy of The Jagarts Collection)

noticing about Lloyd's work was that he was developing a breezy style of acting that made the audience connect with him. Now that he was a contract employee, Fox wanted to exploit this quality. For that reason they pulled him from an assignment in a forthcoming big-budget oater, *Western Union*, to further this character development. And for both Lloyd and Fox, it turned out to be something very special.

As Michael Shayne with Joan Valerie

CHAPTER 9
Michael Shayne

One of the staples of the Hollywood "B" film was the series picture. Ironically, one of the first series began as an "A" production in 1934. MGM was looking to film a Dashiell Hammett novel as quickly as possible. They assigned W.S. Van Dyke, a director with a talent for doing things quickly and under budget, and teamed up newly-acquired William Powell and leading lady Myrna Loy as a husband-and-wife couple. Prior to this project, Powell and Loy had played a married couple in *Manhattan Melodrama*, but Loy's true love in the film was played by Clark Gable. Surrounded by a great script by Albert Hackett and Frances Goodrich, and a great supporting cast, Van Dyke shot the entire film in sixteen days, including retakes. The result was *The Thin Man*. It turned out to be a major success, spawning follow-up films every two or three years.

Fox had tried their hand at series films with Earl Derr Biggers' Charlie Chan even before Nick and Nora Charles were ever dreamed up. Swedish actor Warner Oland played Chan for the first time in 1931 in *Charlie Chan Carries On* (1931), and played the role until his death in 1938. While the Chans were moderately successful in the beginning, they really didn't take off until Robert Ellis and Helen

Logan took over the writing with *Charlie Chan in Egypt* (1935) and Charlie got a number-one son, with Keye Luke assuming the part in *Charlie Chan in Paris* (1934).

Fox was one of the biggest proponents of series films in the thirties. Besides Chan, they produced the Mr. Moto series, with Peter Lorre in the title role, The Jones Family, with Jed Prouty and Spring Byington in the leads, and The Cisco Kid, with Cesar Romero playing the Kid and Chris-Pin Martin as his partner Gordito. (Cisco had been previously filmed by Fox as *In Old Arizona* (1928), with Warner Baxter winning an Academy Award for his performance, and a follow-up by Baxter in *The Cisco Kid* (1931) with Martin appearing as Gordito.)

Still, Fox was looking for a contemporary hero to match Columbia's *Ellery Queen, Boston Blackie, The Lone Wolf* and *Crime Doctor*. RKO also had a successful series going with *The Saint*. They had tried one with the character Barney Callahan, a newspaper reporter played by Michael Whalen. The problem was that Whalen had no on-screen charisma and Fox stopped making Callahan films after three episodes.

Davis Dresser was born in Chicago in 1904, but grew up in West Texas. He lost an eye due to a boyhood accident and was forced to wear an eye patch for the rest of his life. Leading a rough-and-tumble life in his formative years, he settled down to writing in 1927, adopting several pseudonyms, one of them Brett Halliday, which he used for his detective creation Michael Shayne.

It took four years and twenty-two rejections before Henry Holt & Company agreed to publish the first Shayne novel, *Dividend on Death*. This novel was authored under the pen name of Asa Baker. Halliday was one of the characters in the novel, becoming a murder suspect, and he turns to his friend Mike Shayne.

The book was well-received and Halliday quickly wrote a follow-up, *The Private Practice of Michael Shayne,* this time becoming the author instead one of the characters. It was a commercial success.

Physically, Mike Shayne was a tall Irishman who had worked for a large detective agency in New York. He moved to Miami (which was interesting because Halliday lived in Southern California). Halliday modeled Shayne after a tall red-headed American whom he had met in a Tampico bar.

Fox liked *Dividend on Death.* They planned to film using the title of the second book, *The Private Practice of Michael Shayne.* Screenwriters Stanley Rauh and Manning O'Connor capitalized on Lloyd's breezy style, creating a character almost the antithesis of Halliday's creation, and eventually called it *Michael Shayne, Private Detective.* They had a great flair for humor as opposed to comedy relief, and Lloyd pulled it off. An early scene would set the scene for the entire series. It begins with Shayne sitting in his office when two repo men come in to take the furniture. As they move the unpaid items out, Shayne gets a call from a prospective client and tells the men he has a job. They say no money, no chairs, and out the door they go, leaving Shayne in a bare office. Other scenes are Shayne calling Police Captain Painter (a typically bellowing Donald MacBride) using an Italian accent, and when Shayne gets help from Aunt Olivia (a wonderful Elizabeth Patterson), he subtly offers to split the reward with her. Those vignettes are priceless.

In *Michael Shayne, Private Detective* the gumshoe is hired to be a babysitter for Racing Commissioner Hiram Brighton's (Clarence Kolb) spoiled daughter Phyllis (Marjorie Weaver), who escapes from the family mansion to visit Benny Gordon's (Douglass Dumbrille) gambling casino. Trailing Phyllis to the casino, Shayne encounters

Lloyd and Elizabeth Patterson checking out
clues in *Michael Shayne, Private Detective*

Harry Grange (George Meeker), a gambler who has welched on a big
bet. Grange is murdered, Shayne is suspected, and it's up to Phyllis,
Aunt Olivia and Shayne to solve the murder.

It was obvious to the viewer that Lloyd enjoyed starring in the
film *Michael Shayne, Private Detective* as the hilariously wisecracking
title character. His ability to change from a breezy, funny character to
tough guy in a matter of film frames was believable. Shayne, as played
by Lloyd, was the first screen investigator who was portrayed as anything less than a gentleman, and Lloyd had fun with the character.
Eugene Forde's direction had just the right touch. The film was a major success and justified "B" unit Executive Producer Sol M Wurtzel's
decision to continue with the series.

Lloyd and Marjorie Weaver in *Michael Shayne, Private Detective*

Film historian Gary Giddins appreciated the subtlety of Nolan's work on the Shayne film. "Lloyd Nolan could throw a convincing haymaker and rejoinder, but he was always too normal, too average to fit a stereotype. Everything about him was distinct—voice, face, laugh, and line readings—but most distinct was his lack of distinction. He stole scenes by standing around, looking very real, as though a human being had somehow sneaked into a passel of actors. No one was better at making small talk sound like small talk. Intentionally or not, he captured the casual, almost incidental virility of the Halliday character. Watch Nolan's characteristic entrance in *Sleepers West*, as he strolls through a train station (a rare location shot, in Inglewood), twirling a key chain, amiable, unhurried, unconcerned, stopping at a magazine stand, bantering, meeting an old flame, bantering again, and heading for his train, giving no sign that he's on a case. Unlike most B-movie sleuths, Shayne wasn't burdened by a slow-witted pal or excessive comic relief, because Nolan was naturally witty—his voice is a tranquilizing foghorn, nasal yet musical, and his laugh a jaunty teeth-baring sneeze. He was by no means handsome, but he had charm and knew how to wear a fedora."

While moving on with Shayne, Fox dispensed with using any further Halliday work. From then on the remaining six Shayne films would be taken from works of other writers. The second film in the series, *Sleepers West,* was originally not scheduled to be a Shayne. This was a remake of a Preston Foster-Wynne Gibson film, *Sleepers East,* based on a story by Frederick Nebel. It was originally planned for Dean Jagger, but with the success of the first Shayne film, Jagger's character was given to Lloyd, with Lynn Bari as his co-star and Mary Beth Hughes in support. Bari was supposed to have the Hughes role in the Jagger film, but, due to the previous on-screen chemistry between her and Lloyd, she was promoted to the co-starring role.

The plot concerns Shayne transporting a witness (Ms. Hughes) from Denver to San Francisco. On the way they encounter Shayne's former girlfriend, Kay (Lynn Bari), and other assorted characters. Of course, Shayne brings the witness in and gets his girl back.

While this film has many of the elements of the classic *The Narrow Margin* (1952), the major difference is that *Margin* is entirely set on the train while the Shayne entry does not have that claustrophobia, opting instead for a train wreck. Once again, Eugene Forde did a good directing job and the supporting cast, which included Louis Jean Heydt, Don Costello, Don Douglas, and Edward Brophy, acquitted themselves well.

**Michael Shayne shows Otto Kuhn (Erwin Kalser)
how a murder was committed in *Dressed to Kill***

Shayne's next case was *Dressed to Kill,* taken from a yet-to-be-published novel by Richard Burke. This time Mary Beth Hughes played Mike's girlfriend as the couple is headed for the altar when Mike hears a scream in a theater adjacent to her hotel where Shayne is picking her up. Rather then continuing on his way, Shayne investigates and eventually figures things out. Once again Eugene Forde directs the more-than-capable supporting cast with William Demarest standing out as a cop.

Writer Borden Chase's short story *Blue, White, and Perfect* was the basis for Mike's fourth adventure. Chase, who later became known for writing some of the best westerns in film history (*Red River, Winchester '73, The Man from Colorado, Vera Cruz*), was born Frank Fowler in Brooklyn, New York. He took his name from a local dairy. (Borden's milk was the most popular dairy product in New York in those

Al Kikume tries to beat Lloyd at cards in *Blue, White and Perfect.*

days.) Chase migrated to Encino so he could be near the studios. *Blue White and Perfect* was the fourth time a story of his was filmed.

While the story was written in 1937, it was updated for World War II purposes. Once again Shayne's girlfriend Merle (Mary Beth Hughes again) wants Mike to give up being a private eye. She is delighted when Mike tells her he is going to work in an aircraft factory. He learns that industrial diamonds are stolen and are being smuggled out of the country on a boat headed to Hawaii. Mike cons his girl out of $1,000 and gets on the boat. There he meets another old girlfriend (Helene Reynolds) and a suspected spy, Juan Arturo O'Hara (George Reeves). Mike catches the crooks, Merle meets him in Hawaii and when Mike is proclaimed a hero, he and Merle plan to marry.

In his first attempt at a Shayne film, director Herbert I. Leeds

Lloyd romances Mary Beth Hughes in *Blue, White and Perfect*

makes this entry very topical. The scent of patriotism is evident throughout and Lloyd's Shayne does as much to help the war effort as any of the soldiers that Hollywood would portray.

It was back to a straight mystery caper in the next Shayne, *The Man Who Wouldn't Die*, which had a lot more comedy, making up for a weak script adapted from a novel, *No Coffin for the Corpse,* by Clayton Rawson. This time Shayne is *married.* No, not really, just posing as an old girlfriend's (Marjorie Weaver) current husband, trying to find out why she was shot at. The funniest moment is the last scene when Shayne walks down a long flight of stairs, then decides to slide down the banister. All of a sudden he can't stop, he slides out of the frame, and you hear a crash. Fadeout. Herbert I. Leeds was once again at the helm of this adventure, with Henry Wilcoxon, Olin Howland and Helene Reynolds in support.

With Marjorie Weaver in *The Man Who Wouldn't Die*

Series writer Arnaud Dusseau came up with an original screenplay for *Just off Broadway,* the next Shayne film, again with the emphasis on humor. *The New York Times* review put the story in perspective: "It is hard to imagine how any lawyer, even the movie kind, would be so lax as to tolerate Michael Shayne, the series sleuth, on a jury." Yet that is where Mr. Shayne, in the familiar person of Lloyd Nolan, happens to be. While serving on a murder jury one of the witnesses is killed in the courtroom. Mike escapes from the sequestering hotel with the help of an old girlfriend (Marjorie Weaver). He is also saddled with a meddling photographer (Phil Silvers). Mike solves the crime, identifies the murderer, and is given sixty days in jail for leaving the hotel. This was Leeds' third straight Shayne film and, even if the series was beginning to show wears around the edges, Lloyd was still giving a good performance as the breezy gumshoe. *The Hollywood Reporter* remarked, "It was chiefly Nolan who made the release in the series entertaining." *The Daily Variety* echoed, "Nolan fits solidly into the Shayne character adding a lightly humorous touch to the melodramatics."

The final entry would be *Time to Kill* (1943), based on a Raymond Chandler Philip Marlowe story, *The High Window*. Another of Chandler's Marlowe stories was used as the basis for a series film a year earlier. That was *Farewell, My Lovely*, transformed into *The Falcon Takes Over*. It would be remade three years later as *Murder, My Sweet*, a film that forever changed the on-screen persona of Dick Powell. Robert Mitchum played Marlowe in a 1975 film using the novel's original title. *The High Window* would also be made as a Marlowe film in 1947 with George Montgomery playing Chandler's protagonist. It was called *The Brasher Doubloon*. In the Shayne version of the Chandler story, Shayne is hired by a Mrs. Murdock to retrieve a stolen Brasher Doubloon. Of course, there's murder (a few of them) and Shayne straightens out the convoluted story at the end.

The Chandler plot was a good one for Shayne and director Herbert I Leeds. The supporting cast was good, too, with Heather Angel, Ralph Byrd, Doris Merrick and Sheila Bromley lending support. It was be a good swan song for Lloyd as Michael Shayne. His relationship to a Raymond Chandler story was not over, though.

Fox wanted to continue with the Shaynes, and Lloyd was in their plans for at least two more Shayne films. But with World War II being fought and stars like Tyrone Power, Henry Fonda and Victor Mature leaving the screen for the military, Lloyd, who, at thirty-nine years old, was too old to serve, would be promoted to leading-man status.

It wasn't over for Michael Shayne, though. In 1946, Producers Releasing Corporation (PRC), a low-level Poverty Row studio, even

Radio, another venue for Lloyd. Here, going over the
script with Vincent Price for his *Suspense* broadcast

below the status of Republic or Monogram, took a crack at the series.
The PRC Shayne series was more faithful to Halliday's work. Three
of the five PRC Shaynes were based on Halliday novels. Hugh Beau-
mont, later to become famous as Ward Cleaver in the *Leave it to Beaver*
classic television series, was Shayne, Phyllis Hamilton, Shayne's Girl
Friday in the novels, was added to the cast of the PRC films. Cheryl
Walker played her in three films, Kathryn Adams and Trudy Marshall
in one each. Shayne's base of operations appeared to be Los Angeles.
(Lloyd's Michael, for the most part, operated in New York, though
Michael Shayne, Private Detective seemed to be set somewhere else,
possibly Miami Beach, where Halliday's book character resided.)

PRC was not Fox, however, and the lower budgets showed. The series lasted two years, then the films were cut down to thirty minutes in the early fifties for television broadcast.

Shayne also was on radio in various issues throughout the forties and fifties. Wally Maher, a great radio character actor, played Shayne in a syndicated series beginning in 1944. In 1948, Mutual radio brought Shayne back to the airwaves with an up-and-coming star Jeff Chandler in the title role. In the early fifties, both Donald Curtis and Robert Sterling played Shayne on radio as well. Shayne was not through with television though. In 1958 Mark Stevens directed and starred in a TV pilot. Merry Anders played Lucy Hamilton his secretary. Nobody picked up the series, but two years later Four Star Productions, headed by Dick Powell, sold NBC television on a series. Richard Denning played Shayne. Denning, who had been at Paramount when Lloyd had been there, appeared in several of Lloyd's films. He came up through the ranks of "B" films, occasionally getting an "A" role in the 1942 version of Dashiell Hammett's *The Glass Key*. On Radio Denning co starred in two significant series. The first began in 1948 and was called *My Favorite Husband,* and Denning played the straight-laced hubby to an off-the-wall wife played by Lucille Ball. Lucy would take this character to television with her real-life husband, Desi Arnaz, and the show became *I Love Lucy.* When Lucy went to TV, Denning joined with Barbara Britton to play another married couple, *Mr and Mrs North.* Gracie Allen (in a rare appearance without George Burns) and William Post, Jr., originated the married couple in a 1942 MGM film with Gracie as her ditzy self and and Post getting more than he bargained for. The series began shortly thereafter with Alice Frost and Joseph Curtin in the title roles. In the early fifties, many popular radio programs went to TV but continued to do radio as well. *Dragnet* was a great example, so was *Mr. District Attorney.* When Mr. and Mrs. North went to the screen, the Denning-Britton combination was used and they continued to do radio episodes as well.

Denning was a natural for the show, which used Miami Beach for a locale. (The lucky Mr Denning then went on to another envious locale, Hawaii, for the smash series *Hawaii 5-0)* Four Star gave him a great cast of regulars, including veteran character actors Herbert Rudley as Lt Gentry, and Jerry Paris as Newspaperman Tim Rourke. Patricia Donahue, a TV veteran, played Lucy Hamilton and Gary Clarke played her brother, Dick. As a practice, Four Star loaded the episodes with gorgeous women. Among them were Yvonne Craig, Julie Adams, Lola Albright, and Julie London. The series had major problems, though. Rudley, Paris and Ms Donahue were replaced midway through the shoe and Clarke was fired. The show lasted one season.

There would be one last movie hurrah for Michael Shayne, of sorts. It was in 2005 in a film called *Kiss Kiss, Bang Bang,* based on the 1942 Shayne mystery *Bodies Are Where You Find Them.* In true spirit to the Nolan Shaynes, this is played for laughs. Val Kilmer is the detective, this time named Gay Perry (to point out his sexual orientation). The film received great notices.

As for Shayne, he would stay in print until the mid-seventies, a staple of the mystery genre. Lloyd would never make another movie series. But as the fifties came and television became popular, the Shayne series made Lloyd very well prepared to play a recurring character.

CHAPTER 10

The Versatile Mr. Nolan

During the making of the seven Shaynes, Lloyd was getting other work at different studios. For Republic he played a cynical reporter in *Behind the News*. It would be remade in 1955 as *Headline Hunters* with Rod Cameron in Lloyd's role. Over at Universal, for the first time in his career, Lloyd played a baseball player involved in a murder in *Mr.*

With Irene Hervey and young Ann Gillis in *Mr. Dynamite*

Dynamite. Irene Hervey was his female co-star. The screenplay was written by Stanley Rubin, who later became a producer of such films as *The Narrow Margin, Destination Gobi* and *River of No Return.*

Back at his old homestead, Paramount, with his buddy from the Shayne series, director Eugene Forde, Lloyd played a racketeer taking over a small-town jail and making it a luxury hotel for gangsters in the comedy *Buy Me That Town.*

For the first time since his first film, *"G" Men,* Lloyd went back to Warner Bros. Even though, by this time Lloyd had perfected his easygoing, humorous type of character on both sides of the law, Lloyd was truly villainous in *Blues in the Night.* Richard Whorf stars as "Jigger" Pine, a pianist who forms a blues band with his friends, Leo Powell, a trumpeter (Jack Carson), his wife "Character," a singer (Priscilla

L-R Warren Hymer, Constance Moore, Lloyd,
Albert Dekker in *Buy Me That Town*

Lane), Peppi, a drummer (Billy Halop), Pete Bassett, a bassist (Peter Whitney), and clarinetist Nicky Haroyan (Elia Kazan). The group plays all over the south, traveling by boxcar. One day they encounter an escaped criminal, Del Davis (Lloyd), who befriends the group. He gets them a job in a New Jersey roadhouse with Davis' girlfriend, Kay (Betty Field), and former partners Brad Ames (Wallace Ford) and Sam Paryas (Howard Da Silva). Leo makes a play for Kay, but goes back to Character when he finds out she's pregnant. When Character has to stop singing due to her condition, Jigger hires Kay as a replacement and falls in love with her. The pair runs away and Jigger hits the skids after he finds out that Kay has been using him. Kay returns to Del and begs him to take her back, but Davis refuses. Kay shoots Del, and then is taken away by Brad, who kills them both in a suicidal automobile wreck.

The film, originally called *Hot Nocturne,* had a great score, including the title song written by Harold Arlen and Johnny Mercer. It was originally written for James Cagney, and then Dennis Morgan was considered as his replacement. John Garfield was also considered before director Anatole Litvak settled on Whorf. Whorf would go on to a directing career, though not as famous as his co-player, Elia Kazan. Others considered for roles in the film were Barbara Stanwyck, Rita Hayworth, Claire Trevor, William Holden, and Nick (Richard) Conte.

Despite not having as much screen time as the others, Lloyd was billed fourth. It was the first time he ever had to get rough with a beautiful girl on screen, as he had to hit Betty Field in the film. He remembered, "Trying to hit Betty without hurting her and still have the slap look real was one of the most difficult assignments I've ever tackled. As a matter of fact, she had every right to shoot the so and so I played in the picture." Lloyd's work, once again, was appreciated by *The Hollywood Reporter* who wrote, "Lloyd's gangster is alternately terrifying and docile—a good job." Considering that Lloyd got the part over Garfield, Bogart and Raft, who were among the others considered for the part, it was quite a compliment.

Another programmer at Warner Bros., *Steel Against the Sky*, had Lloyd and Craig Stevens as brothers fighting for the hand of Alexis Smith. Stevens got her at the end, as well as in real life. Back at Fox, Lloyd played the manager of the Brooklyn baseball team in *It Happened in Flatbush*. In *Manila Calling*, another film directed by Herbert I Leeds, Lloyd and Cornel Wilde took on parts originally meant for Pat O'Brien and Dana Andrews. Preston Foster was also considered for Lloyd's role. In this action drama, Lloyd and Wilde battle for the hand of a stranded dancer (Carole Landis) and try to save Manila. This time, Lloyd gets the girl.

And what a girl he got! Carole Landis in *Manila Calling*

Lloyd wrapped up his between-the-Shaynes era back at MGM with *Apache Trail*, a good brother-bad brother film. Lloyd is bad, William Lundigan is good, and Donna Reed, as a Mexican girl, is pretty.

☆☆☆

Away from the screen, Lloyd enjoyed raising avocados and writing one-act plays. Mell, on the other hand, just loved coarse ground pepper and would season almost every dish with it. She felt that it was much healthier than salt because, while salt was absorbed by the body, pepper came from a plant and, thus, was digested. Then, World War II began. Lloyd's nephew, who was in the intelligence division of the Army Air Corps., urged them to stock up on pepper because the war would make it unavailable for a long time. Mell heeded his suggestion and bought many, many cases of whole peppercorn. As it turned out, they never had to buy pepper again. Those cases would keep them supplied for decades.

The Nolans did their patriotic duty and had a Victory Garden behind the swimming pool.

☆☆☆

After a futile defense of Manila for Fox, Lloyd was one of the participants in another futile battle, that of *Bataan*. Made at MGM and directed by Tay Garnett, this film utilized most of the regulars on the MGM lot. Robert Taylor starred as battle-hardened sergeant Bill Dane. George Murphy, Thomas Mitchell, Lee Bowman, Desi Arnaz, and a very young Robert Walker were others of the ill-fated group on the Peninsula. Lloyd was billed fourth as Corporal Barney Todd (originally assigned to Richard Whorf). Todd was kind of a wise guy with a past; in the film he is the second to last to perish.

Dore Schary was the executive producer of the film and had many issues with it. He had to pay RKO a sum of $6,500 for the rights to use any part of their 1934 John Ford film, *The Lost Patrol*, or run the risk of a lawsuit for copyright infringement. In his autobiography, Schary referred to *Bataan* as a remake of *The Lost Patrol*. (It was, in fact, remade in 1939 as a western, *Bad Lands*. Actually, *The Lost Patrol* of 1934, which starred Victor McLaglen, was a remake of a 1929 British film of the same name, which had starred his brother, Cyril McLaglen.) In addition, Schary had taken a chance using African-American Kenneth Spencer in a significant role of Pvt. Wesley Eeps. The Eeps character was based on real-life Pvt Robert H. Brooks, the first American soldier killed in the Philippines. The film was not shown in certain parts of the American south. Schary was redeemed, however, when the NAACP awarded MGM a scroll of merit, for the film's realism and for showing "how superfluous racial and religious problems are when common danger is faced." In February, 1944, the Junior Council of the NAACP gave MGM a special award for its sympathetic and intelligent portrayal of a black soldier. Many reviews credited *Bataan* as the first film made by Robert Walker when, in fact, he had appeared in three prior films; but this was his first significant role. Walter Pidgeon was announced as the star playing a "Sgt Bill Dever," a "new model sergeant" in the "new model United States Army." The original script had nineteen principals, including a Native American, each representing separate arms of the service. In mid-1942, Robert Young was announced as George Murphy's co-star. This also was the first dramatic role for Desi Arnaz. According to his autobiography, it was he who thought up the idea of his reciting the Mea Culpa confessional prayer in his death scene, a prayer he had learned as a child.

Reviewers were very taken with the film's realism. Writing in the *New York Times*, Bosley Crowther said, "This time, at least, a studio hasn't purposely 'prettified' facts. This time it has made a picture about war in true and ugly detail … There is sickening filth and bloodshed in it." Crowther said on Lloyd, "He comes through nicely at the climax."

From an infamous battle of the Philippines, Lloyd cinematically remained in the Pacific, but it was in quite an opposite setting. This time he played Sgt. "Hook" Malone, a member of the US Marines in *Guadalcanal Diary*, the story of the first US offensive in the Pacific. Another all-star male cast graced this Fox Classic, including Preston Foster as Father Donnelly, William Bendix as Cpl "Taxi" Potts, straight out of Flatbush, Richard Conte as Capt. Davis, and Anthony Quinn as Jesus "Soose" Alvarez. Richard Tregaskis' novel was accurately adapted by Lamar Trotti. Lloyd stands out in the ensemble showing strength, bravery and humor without once ever going over the top. The scenes before the actual invasion, which established the characters, are well done. The battle scenes are realistic.

The majority of the film was shot at Camp Pendleton near Oceanside, California. Many of the Marines stationed there were used as extras, and some actually had speaking parts. Other parts of the film were shot aboard a Navy Transport. Originally, Fox had obtained waivers from Lloyd, Preston Foster, and William Bendix, allowing the opening title card to read, "The United States Marines In Guadalcanal Diary," but the Marines never received any on-screen credit, though the music over the opening credits utilized "From the Halls of Montezuma."

This was Richard Jaeckel's first film. He had been a studio messenger boy before being cast in this film. Anthony Quinn was originally not cast in this film, but was given the role of "Soose" after it was suggested to Fox that it would help the popularity of the US in Latin-American countries if a Latin was portrayed as a hero, as opposed to the customary "heavy." Quinn physically resembled Sgt. Frank Few, an Arizona Indian, who was one of the great heroes of Guadalcanal. Eddie Acuff, as Tex, was based on Gunnery Sgt. Charles E. Angus, a famous Marine marksman whose marksmanship became part of the "Guadalcanal Legend." Victor McLaglen was originally cast as Donnelly; Preston Foster was supposed to be Capt. Cross (Roy Roberts). Later, McLaglen was supposed to play Col. Grayson, but that part went to Minor Watson. The production was responsible for another first: Reed Hadley, playing a correspondent, supplied passages of narration, a device Fox would use in several more films, including one of Lloyd's best.

Lloyd, again, got great notices. *The Hollywood Reporter* loved his interpretation, saying: "Lloyd Nolan gives a grand account of Sgt. Hook Malone."

The film had its premiere in Philadelphia to represent the one-hundred-sixty-eighth anniversary of the Marine Corps and Hollywood, which was a benefit for War Charities.

After appearing in *Bataan* and *Guadalcanal Diary*, Lloyd, beginning to become conscious of his image, rejected two scripts. He turned down *Wing and a Prayer,* where he was considered for the part played by Dana Andrews, and later considered for the role played by Murray Alper, which he thumbed down because he was tired of appearing in war films. Radio, however, was able to coax him to do some acting on the *Results, Inc.* series in 1944 and the award winning *Suspense* where he starred three times in 1945. Fox permitted him to withdraw from the title role in *Roger Touhy, Gangster*—taking a stand against portraying any more on screen gunmen. (Kent Taylor was offered the role of Touhy, with Preston Foster playing his G-Man captor. Subsequently, the roles were reversed.) The rejections could have resulted in suspension, but that would be all right. Lloyd had plenty going on at home to keep him busy. He spent the time working on his house and enjoying his family.

☆☆☆

On February 1, 1943, Mell had given birth to a son. In spite of the Irish tradition of naming the firstborn son after the father, Mell and Lloyd named the baby Jay Benedict Nolan. Their family was now complete.

At first, little Jay appeared to be like other babies, but as time went on, he would show characteristics that made it obvious that he was different. He didn't talk, neither at the expected age, nor any other. He didn't react to external stimuli as other babies did. Was he deaf, they wondered? They had his ears tested. No, his hearing was fine. His parents took him from doctor to doctor, trying to find out what was wrong. As Lloyd would later tell *Los Angeles Times* reporter Ursula Vils, "The first time you go to any knowledgeable doctor—we went to San Francisco, the East, everywhere—you take your son and the first thing the doctor says is, 'How is your marriage doing?'" It was the sad truth in that decade that even the medical professionals would often think that a child whose behavior was peculiar was made that way by bad parenting. Often, a disability such as Jay's was thought back then to be caused by "refrigerator mothers." That has, of course, been disproven since then.

The realization would come later that Jay was not able to under-

A lighthearted moment with costars Cathy Lewis and young Dawn Bender
prior to a 1945 *Suspense* show (Courtesy of Julia Posel)

stand the world, and predictability was what he craved. Routines would be an emotional oasis, for when his environment was predictable, he could enjoy some level of peace.

Throughout her life, big sister Melinda would love her brother and speak of him fondly, even though he was unable to respond in kind.

Mell hired a very kind, but strict, lady named Edna to be their nanny and housekeeper. When Lloyd was performing in plays in Europe, Mell would go visit him. During these times, Edna would live in their home and take care of the children. She, like so many of their employees, would remain with the Nolans for many years.

☆☆☆

Although Lloyd was off the screen for the year 1944, he was working steadily. After he made a couple of war propaganda short films, he learned that his former co-player from *Blues in the Night,* Elia Kazan, had been given his first opportunity to direct a film. Kazan was a member of the Group Theater when Lloyd appeared in an ill-fated Group production, *Gentlewoman.* Kazan had been a member of the Group since 1932 and wrote, directed, and acted there. Although his ultimate dream was to direct, he had to act to pay the bills. His unusual Greek facial features brought him to Warner Bros. for two films, *City for Conquest* and *Blues,* both directed by Anatole Litvak. He played fast-talking Brooklyn-type characters in both. Kazan's first directing project was *A Tree Grows in Brooklyn,* based on the bestselling novel by Betty Smith. The screen rights to the yet-to-be-published novel precipitated a bidding war among several studios. Fox paid $55,000 for the rights and intended to star Alice Faye. When she proved unavailable, Gene Tierney was tested for the lead. Fred MacMurray, and Jeanne Crain were also considered for parts. Fox eventually cast Dorothy McGuire as Katie Nolan, James Dunn as Johnny Nolan Joan Blondell as Aunt Sissy, Lloyd as McShayne, the local cop on the beat, and Peggy Ann Garner in the pivotal role of young Francie Nolan.

A Tree Grows in Brooklyn is the story of an adolescent girl, Francie Nolan, and her relationship with her alcoholic father, Johnny Nolan, always the dreamer, eventually proving to be the ultimate failure. Even though the story contains many elements of the Nolan family, the film was carried by the loving relationship between father and daughter. The thirteen-year-old Miss Garner began acting in films at age seven and handled her role with sensitivity and delicacy. Dunn, on the other hand, had been a leading man at Fox in the early thir-

A scene with Dorothy McGuire and Joan Blondell in
A Tree Grows in Brooklyn, a film that would become a classic

ties, when he drank himself out of there, stumbling to the lower-tier companies like Republic and Monogram. Fox conducted an extensive search for the right man to play Johnny Nolan, and Dunn had to be tested twice, once at the beginning of the search and again when all of the other possibilities had been exhausted. Both Fox and Dunn were ecstatic. He delivered a once-in-a-lifetime performance. The father-daughter characters were so dominant that the other stars of the film, whose parts were not as showy, got lost in the histrionics. An analysis of the film reveals that Lloyd and Joan Blondell do some of the best work of their careers. It would become one of Lloyd's most remembered roles. Dorothy McGuire, in the not-so-sympathetic role of Katie Nolan, was also very believable, even though she was only 13 years older than her on-screen daughter, Peggy Ann Garner.

Kazan did some remarkable work in his directorial debut. He also brought to Hollywood another future director in Nicholas Ray, who essentially was his assistant. Ray was involved in many phases of the film, including appearing in the film as a bakery clerk and working with Alfred Newman on the score.

A Tree Grows in Brooklyn got two Oscar nominations. One was for screenplay; the other was for Dunn's performance as a supporting actor. Dunn won an Oscar but, unfortunately, he was not able to parlay it into a career revival. Peggy Ann Garner was awarded a special Juvenile Oscar for her work in 1945. Her friend, child star Sybil Jason, tells us, "Peggy, bless her, had nothing but the best to say about Lloyd." Then, speaking for herself, Sybil continues, "He seemed like such a noble gentleman."

Thirty years later, when interviewed by Dr. Ronald L. Davis for an SMU Oral History project, Lloyd was asked which of his one-hundred-plus films had been his favorite. His answer was, "I think that possibly the best balanced film would be *A Tree Grows in Brooklyn."* He was not alone. Everybody involved with the project was proud to be associated with it.

Another programmer then came Lloyd's way was *Circumstantial Evidence.* Michael O'Shea stars as a man convicted of murder, based on circumstantial evidence. Lloyd plays a postman who helps in clearing him. John Larkin directed, many of the usual Fox support team were there, including Trudy Marshall, Roy Roberts and Reed Hadley.

For the biopic *Captain Eddie,* Fox assigned Fred MacMurray to play the real-life aviator and automobile pioneer Eddie Rickenbacker, and Lloyd's former on-screen gal-pal, Lynn Bari, to play his wife Adelaide. Rickenbacker's life is told in flashback as he and his crew sits on a life raft after his transport plane crashes in the Pacific. Lloyd played Lt. Jim Whitaker, a real-life survivor. Whitaker, in fact, was credited as a Technical Adviser on the film and would eventually write a book on the incident, as did Rickenbacker.

Rickenbacker, who was a World War I hero, a Congressional Medal of Honor recipient, and later the President of Eastern Airlines, was like the cat with nine lives, having survived a plane crash that left him in a coma for several days in 1941. His life was the stuff that Hollywood biographies are made from. While David O Selznick wanted to make a film on his life, Winfield Sheehan won the bid, reportedly receiving backing from Charles Lindberg. This would be the last production for Sheehan, who, at one time, ran Fox until it merged with Darryl Zanuck's 20th Century Pictures in 1935, with Zanuck taking over the studio. Sheehan had only one production since his last Fox film in 1935 before this opportunity came along. Sheehan died shortly after the film opened in June of 1945. He was only sixty-one. Rickenbacker himself had roadblocks in his life that effected the production.

He was outspoken and had frequently voiced his unpopular views on organized labor. Fox had received a storm of protest when they announced they would make the film. Gary Cooper was Sheehan's original choice to play Rickenbacker, but several unions petitioned Cooper to turn down the role, which he did. The project, which had been scheduled for 1943, was put on the shelf until late 1944. Upon release, the *New York Times* reported the film had "provoked some loud alarm" due to its "hero-worship" portrayal of Rickenbacker. The *Times* also added that "Fred MacMurray looks no more like Rickenbacker than the story resembles his career."

Lloyd's final release of 1945 became one of his signature films, *The House on 92nd Street.* The film was the brainchild of producer Louis de Rochemont. Born in Chelsea, Massachusetts, just before the turn of the century, Louis Clarke de Rochemont shot his first newsreel at the age of twelve. After serving in the Navy following World War I, he became a cameraman for Pathé news, eventually going out on his own and co-founding *The March of Time* newsreel series, along with Roy E. Larsen on Time Inc. in 1934. *The March of Time* shorts were more than just newsreels. They subtly told stories more often than not condemning the Nazi regime. De Rochemont continued to produce the *March of Time* shorts personally until he left for Hollywood. He shot his first full-length feature, *The Ramparts We Watch,* on location in New London, Connecticut, in 1940, using non-professional actors. Another full-length documentary, *We Are the Marines,* narrated by Westbrook Van Voorhis, came two years later. That was followed by the brilliant documentary *The Fighting Lady,* which won him an Oscar for the best documentary. De Rochemont finally got an opportunity to blend documentary style with a Hollywood drama, and the result was *The House on 92ⁿᵈ Street*. The film begins showing actual surveillance footage taken by the F.B.I., with an authentic voiceover by Reed Hadley. The documentary aspect morphs into the story. Throughout the narrative, the film has a realistic feel. Much of the story was filmed in actual locations, such as New York's Columbus Circle, the George Washington Bridge and other places around town. The Bureau's headquarters in Washington, DC was utilized as well. Several members of the Bureau were photographed in the performance of their jobs. To add further realism, many of the principal players were virtual unknowns. The only established players were Lloyd, William Eythe, Signe Hasso, Gene Lockhart, William Post Jr., and Leo G. Carroll. E.G. Marshall, Vincent Gardenia, and Paul Ford all made their screen

In conversation with J. Edgar Hoover between takes, *The House on 92nd Street*. (From the collection of Nolan Lightfoot.)

debuts in this film. They would go on to greater recognition. So would Harry Bellaver, Bruno Wick, Alfred Linder, Charles Waggenheim and Harro Meller, who had been in films before but with very little recognition. And Lydia St Clair was menacing as Johanna Schmidt. This would be the only feature film she would make.

Lloyd played F.B.I. Inspector George A. Briggs, a fictional lieutenant of Director J. Edgar Hoover. He oversees the operation called *The Christopher Case,* a case involving stolen secrets of developmental Process 97, the secret of the Atomic Bomb. De Rochement had some good fortune in this. When principal photography was being done, few in the United States knew about the Atomic Bomb. When the device was dropped on Hiroshima in August of 1945, the film was nearly ready for release. Reed Hadley's narration was adjusted to include the Atomic Bomb as the definition of Process 97 but none of the characters in the film mentions the bomb. A nest of spies ferreted out by a double agent, William Dietrich (William Eythe), and the leader, "Mr. Christopher," is, in reality, Elsa Gebhardt (Signe Hasso). There were very few actors who could have played Briggs. Lloyd's ability to be a natural actor provided the perfect element to make the character fit in with the docu-drama style. One of the highlights of both Lloyd's and William Eythe's career was to be allowed to spend a week at the F.B.I. training academy in Quantico Virginia (which would be used as an on-location venue in the follow-up, *The Street With No Name*).

In the original screenplay, "Mr. Christopher" was to be a man, playing a woman (Elsa), creating the illusion that the character would be the least-suspected person on the screen Darryl Zanuck conducted an extensive search for an unknown stage actor before deciding to reverse the gender and use Ms. Hasso. Kurt Katch was assigned to play Col. Felix

Strassen, but was replaced by actor-director Alfred Zeisler. Many of the characters of this production were based on real-life people. Bill Dietrich was based on William G. Sebold, a German-born American citizen, who infiltrated a spy ring with the aid of the F.B.I. and set up a shortwave radio station. Elsa Gebhardt was modeled after socialite Lilly Stein, who wound up being convicted of espionage. Col. Hammersohn was close to Frederick Joubert Duquesne, one of Germany's most famous spies, who ran a New York City spy ring, which tried to steal the plans for the Norden bombsite. Duquesne had been a professional spy for over forty years at the time of his arrest. Hermann Lang, who memorized details of the Norden bombsight, was the inspiration for "Charles Ogden Roper" (Gene Lockhart). The real-life spies received multi-year sentences.

The House on 92nd Street received uniformly excellent notices. The New York Times singled out Lloyd by saying, "The FBI agents, other than Mr. Nolan, are genuine and his performance is so restrained and unimposing in a theatrical sense that one accepts his Inspector Briggs as being the real thing." Once again, Lloyd was involved in a project that was a feather in the cap for everyone involved, most importantly Charles G Booth, who won an Oscar for best original screenplay. Lloyd played the character again three years later in The Street With No Name. Lloyd and Signe Hasso would recreate their roles on Radio's Screen Guild Players; William Lundigan was Dietrich. Humphrey Bogart would play the Briggs role in a 1952 radio play broadcast on Stars on the Air with Keefe Brasselle as Dietrich. As for de Rochemont, the success of 92nd Street established both him and his style of filmmaking. For the next decade, de Rochemont produced a handful of brilliant documentaries and docudramas, the highlight being Boomerang! Other producers picked up on this style; the most famous was Mark Hellinger, who made The Naked City entirely on location in New York City.

Two Smart People (a.k.a. *Time for Two*), with John Hodiak and Lucille Ball

Lloyd had two releases in 1946. Shot first, but released much later, was *Two Smart People,* an MGM release directed by Jules Dassin. This confusing comedy-drama was Dassin's last under his MGM contract, which they would not renew. It was a grave misstep for Leo the Lion and Company as Dassin went with Mark Hellinger to direct *Brute Force* and *The Naked City,* becoming a top-tier director before having to flee the country to avoid appearing before the HUAC. Lloyd plays a cop out to bring back a confidence man (John Hodiak) who meets a confidence lady (Lucille Ball), and all sorts of complications ensue.

A casual observer on the set noticed that Nolan was merely sitting quietly instead of engaging in his co-stars' playfulness. Why? Doesn't he have any temperament, the visitor asked director Jules Dassin. "No Temperament? Why he's the most temperamental actor in Hollywood. He's an actor's actor, a complete master of his art," Dassin responded. "But he doesn't waste his temperament throwing fits. He puts it into his work."

Lloyd was back with Hodiak in his other 1946 film, *Somewhere in the Night*. This vastly-underrated film, the second directorial effort of Joseph L Mankiewicz, is pure *film noir*. Hodiak, in one of his best performances, plays a soldier with amnesia looking to find out his past and wishing he hadn't. He is helped by nightclub singer Christy Smith (Nancy Guild), making her screen debut after being spotted in a *Life* magazine article about the University of Arizona. Lloyd plays a cop again, this time a very cerebral and sensitive one. Lloyd has great fun with some of his lines, especially those making fun of movie cops. Ironically, his last line bails movie cops out. Richard Conte, excellent in a co-starring role, completes the leading quartet.

Lloyd would complete the cinematic cop trifecta but, in his next film, he was anything but an honest cop. The film was *Lady in the Lake*, based on the Raymond Chandler novel featuring his Philip Marlowe. Robert Montgomery starred as Marlowe and directed this unusual film as well. As most film buffs know, *Lady in the Lake* (1947) was shot directly entirely with a subjective camera. The only time you saw the hero, Marlowe, was when he looked in a mirror or when he interrupted the narrative to bring the viewer up to date in a head shot. This exercise in filmmaking presented an entirely new set of problems for the cast, which included Audrey Totter, Leon Ames, Jayne Meadows, Tom Tully and Lloyd. Actors are instinctively trained to look away from the camera so performing in this film was a violation of all the rules. The plot has Marlowe as a writer being invited by a publishing company's female editor (Audrey Totter) ostensibly to negotiate a contract for his literary work, but in reality being hired to look for the publisher's (Leon Ames) philandering wife. Marlowe (a.k.a. the camera) finds himself framed for murder, slugged, jailed, beaten and nearly killed by the crooked cop, DaGarmot (Lloyd). The film was set around Christmas time, which seemed to be an incongruous and an unnecessary plot device. Critics were divided on the first-person camera technique. Many felt that it slowed the plot down. *The New York Times* observed, "In making the camera an active participant, rather than an off side reporter, Mr. Montgomery has, however, failed to exploit the full possibilities suggested by this unusual technique. For after a few minutes of seeing a hand reaching toward a door knob, or lighting a cigarette or lifting a glass, or a door moving toward you as though it might come right out of the screen the novelty begins to wear thin." However, *Variety* complimented the technique by pointing out, "The idea comes off excellently, transferring what otherwise would have been a fair whodunit into socko screen fare." Lloyd seemed to benefit the most from the subjective camera. He looked more natural acting to the lens than did some of the others, who looked wooden at times. Much of that can be attributed to his stage training where an actor often looks to an audience. *The Hollywood Reporter* agreed, "Lloyd Nolan has never been more expert than he is in delivering his role of Police Lt. DaGarmot." So did the *Daily Variety*: "Lloyd Nolan does some stand-out work as the tough and crooked copper who is the main heavy of the piece."

The film was not without its dangers, though. In an interview printed in Doug McClelland's book, *Forties Film Talk,* Lloyd remembered, "I almost lost an eye on that picture. I'm supposed to be shot by a gun fired from outside the window on a fire escape. They had to physically shoot a gun pellet through the glass to get the splintering effect. The pellet ricocheted at a 90-degree angle. One piece flew into my eye actually curving around the cornea. They rushed me to a hospital where a doctor removed it."

This was Montgomery's first full film as a director. He had directed some of *They Were Expendable* when John Ford was sidelined with a fractured leg, suffered in a fall on the set. The film was a melancholy one for Montgomery, as it was his last at a studio he called home since 1929. Again, Leo and Company's timing was a bit off. Montgomery went to Universal and his next film, *Ride the Pink Horse,* which again he both directed and starred, was hailed as a masterpiece. A few years later, Montgomery retired from acting and, like his Philip Marlowe predecessor, Dick Powell, became a television pioneer and executive.

☆☆☆

After a five-year absence, Lloyd returned to his first home, Paramount, to co-star with Alan Ladd and Robert Preston in *Wild Harvest,* his other 1947 film. A lot had changed at the Marathon Street studio since Lloyd was last there. Alan Ladd, who was picking up day work wherever he could (one of those roles was in the last scene of the legendary *Citizen Kane*), made his unofficial screen introduction as a killer in *This Gun for Hire* and immediately became a star. Now he was king of the lot. The diminutive Ladd was energy, intensity and sex, all rolled up into a small package. Tay Garnett tried to make this film into a Howard Hawksian story about man's loyalty to men. Ladd, Preston and Nolan are part of a harvesting crew. Dorothy Lamour, in what was advertised as her first dramatic role, marries Preston to be close to Ladd. At the conclusion, the male threesome walk away together, leaving Lamour alone to find another guy.

Mell's byline appeared on an article entitled "The Man I Married," in reference to his 1940 film, in the December, 1948, issue of *Silver Screen* magazine. In this piece, she explained how different Lloyd was from his outlaw or stone-faced authority-figure characters. "He is a good husband. He is one of the gentlest men I ever met. He's a little quiet, very amusing, very kind, and very attractive," she wrote. "He is also superb as a father to our seven-year-old Melinda and five-year-old Jay." Mell described his sentimentality, never forgetting birthdays and anniversaries, and happily buying presents and flowers. He was also a silly-note writer, leaving them all over the house. When he was working out of town, he would leave notes for Mell in places she would be sure to go—places like the linen closet or her stationery box—and he used to call her every night until their business manager put his foot down. Then their calls were reduced to every other night. When Lloyd was working in town, he'd call every day, usually in late morning. One thing he enjoyed buying for himself was unusual ties.

Mell and Lloyd both loved meeting his fans in small towns because they were so warm, courteous, and friendly. Around this movie star, they behaved with dignity. How that was appreciated.

She said that Lloyd tended to be too nice sometimes, so they hired an agent to handle with more aggressiveness those things that required it.

There were three things about Lloyd that drove Mell bananas, though: 1) he could fall asleep anytime, anywhere while she had to "psyche herself up" to sleep, 2) if he wasn't hungry, there was no way they could get him to eat, and 3) he would catch planes and trains at the very last minute. In spite of that, she said he was "my idea of the best husband in the world."

From all indications, it seems the feeling was quite mutual.

☆☆☆

1948 was a significant year for the motion picture industry. An act of Congress forced the studios to divest themselves of their own theater chains. Studios were getting rid of their highly-paid stars, and television was starting to get a post-war push. The major studios reduced or dropped "B" and programming pictures. Universal dropped serial features and, within a decade, the two remaining chapter-play studios, Republic and Columbia, followed suit. When an actor could make four or five pictures a year in the years up to the end of World War II, the same actor was lucky now to get two.

1948 was the third straight year that Lloyd had a pair of features. The first was *Green Grass of Wyoming* for Fox. This was the third in the Mary O'Hara Horse Trilogy; Ms. O'Hara had scored with *My Friend Flicka* in 1943. Roddy McDowall played young Ken McLaughlin, with Preston Foster and Rita Johnson playing his parents. Two years later, the three reunited for a sequel, *Thunderhead, Son of Flicka.* This effort was to be the third installment of the series. Fox wanted to reunite the three leads again, but they had gone their separate ways. Instead, they cast twenty-three-year-old Robert Arthur, who would prove to be a standout in both *Twelve O'Clock High* and *Ace In The Hole* later on in his career. Playing his parents were Lloyd and Geraldine Wall. Charles Coburn was on hand as a drunken ex-trainer, and British import Peggy Cummins was cast as Arthur's love interest. They all played second fiddle to the horse set, led by lovers Thunderhead and the newest McLaughlin mare, Crown Jewels.

In an interview published in 1992, Robert Arthur found making the film an unpleasant experience. He told Doug McClelland, "*Green Grass* was a tough picture to make. Louis King, the director, was a very nervous man, and the whole production seemed jumpy and tense. Peggy Cummins was my leading lady. She was rude, flippant and generally unpleasant. When I was first brought to Peggy on the set, someone said, 'Miss Cummins, I'd like you to meet Robert Arthur, your leading man.' And she growled, 'I look like his muthah!' The chemistry couldn't have been worse." The best thing about the film was the Technicolor photography, which won Charles G. Clarke an Oscar nomination. The film did make money.

Lloyd would reprise his role of Inspector George A. Briggs in Fox's follow-up to *The House on 92nd Street,* the *film noir, The Street With No Name.* Louis de Rochemont was not involved with this one; Samuel G. Engel produced it and William Keighley directed. Many of de Rochemont's semi-documentary touches were missing. There was a scene set at the F.B.I. Training Academy in Quantico, Virginia, but the story itself was more linear. Mark Stevens plays undercover F.B.I. agent Eugene Cordell, assigned to break up a gang led by Alex Stiles (Richard Widmark, who was coming off a brilliant performance as a psychotic killer in *Kiss of Death*). Widmark still inserts many of his psychotic components into his interpretation of Stiles. There is also a traitor cop in the midst. Ed Begley, Barbara Lawrence, future director Joseph Pevney, Donald Buka, and John McIntyre provided good support. Lloyd, Widmark and Stevens recreated their roles on a January, 1949, *Lux Radio Theater.* Stevens and Stephen McNally would do the story on *Lux* again that December. The plot would be reused in 1955 for Samuel Fuller's *House of Bamboo,* set in Tokyo, with Robert Stack as the undercover cop and Robert Ryan in the Widmark role. Ryan

With Claude Jarman, Jr., in *The Sun Comes Up*

was more psychotic than Widmark, but he underplayed the role so well, he was far more effective. Biff Elliott was originally supposed to play a pseudo-Inspector Briggs, but Brad Dexter was given the part instead. Elliott would play a member of Ryan's gang.

Came 1949 and Lloyd was back to co-starring with an animal, this time screendom's most famous canine, Lassie, in MGM's *The Sun Comes Up*. The original story was written by Marjorie Kinnan Rawlings, who had written *The Yearling*, a major triumph for MGM in 1946. Claude Jarman, who scored in the role of Jody in that classic, was once again prominent in this one. Jeanette MacDonald was the human lead. This was pure soap opera with Miss MacDonald playing Helen Lorfield Winter, a widowed singer, who then loses her son when he is hit by a truck chasing after his dog (Lassie). She runs away to a secluded small California coastal town where she meets a local writer (Lloyd) and Jerry, an orphan boy (Jarman). Helen rejects Jerry and Lassie, but the collie saves the day, the boy and Helen. Ms. MacDonald has some good numbers, but the story was from four-hankie ville. Once a major star at Paramount and MGM, Jeanette felt that she had hit bottom in this, playing second fiddle to a four-legged legend. She quit films after this one.

Next, Lloyd co-starred with Audie Murphy in the latter's first starring movie role. Entitled *Bad Boy*, this 1949 film is about a juvenile delinquent, Danny, who is sent to the Variety Club Ranch. Lloyd's character is the wise, patient marshal who discovers that it was Danny's erroneous notion that he was the cause of his mother's death that triggered his criminal behavior. In real life, Lloyd knew about Murphy's sad history and felt very sorry for him. Even though Murphy was the most-decorated soldier in World War II and cited for enormous brav-

Jane Wyatt and Lloyd in *Bad Boy*

ery, the man would suffer greatly from what is known now as post-traumatic stress syndrome. He often carried a gun with him and had a temper that could go off at any time. Lloyd wondered if the root of Audie's odd behavior could be similar to that of Danny's—someone's death, for which he felt responsible. In Murphy's case, it could be the deaths of over two hundred enemy soldiers. Lloyd suspected that he was having flashbacks of his encounters with those doomed men.

Lloyd closed the decade with a supporting role in *Easy Living*. He plays the owner of a football team on which Victor Mature is the star. Mature's Pete Wilson does not tell anybody he has a heart condition. His wife (Lizabeth Scott) is a status seeker who won't put up with Pete's falling star. Lucille Ball, making her first RKO picture in seven years (she would eventually buy the studio), plays Lloyd's daughter,

Lloyd surrounded by Kenny Washington (1) and
other members of the Los Angeles Rams in *Easy Living*

who is in love with Mature. Sonny Tufts, Paul Stewart and Dick Erd-
man were among the co-stars. Also appearing in the film was Kenny
Washington, the second African-American NFL football player
(Woody Strode, who also became an actor, was the first), and several
members of the Los Angeles Rams. Jacques Tourneur directed the
film, an interesting choice as, prior to getting the assignment, he had
never seen a football game. Tourneur also used a baseball park (Wrig-
ley Field in Los Angeles) for the football scenes.

1949 also brought Lloyd an honor unlike no other. In June, the
Parents League of America voted him "Movie Father of the Year." This
special plaque was awarded to him for two reasons: "His numerous
portrayals of the ideal father on the screen" and also his "home life

Lloyd, Jay and Melinda in a slightly different pose, but taken during the same session. Photographer—Murray Garrett, Herald Examiner Collection/Los Angeles Public Library.

is typical of the happy American family." The photograph that accompanied the announcement in the *Los Angeles Daily News* showed Melinda looking on as Lloyd was feeding Jay. Photographer Murray Garrett, who took that picture, remembers the Nolans as a wonderful family. When he arrived at their house that day, their warm welcome made him feel like a friend, not an intruder. He was pleased to see that, even though Jay was quite disabled, he was included in everything the family did. Lloyd and Mell, he felt, were completely family-oriented. Garrett was also impressed by the respect that Lloyd and Mell had for each other. You don't see that very much in the world of showbiz.

Contrary to what the Parents League of America thought, however, the Nolans' home life was far from typical. Lloyd was so proud of his children; but Jay required more of his parents' attention than most children would. While he hadn't gone public yet with this daunting challenge, Lloyd did keep his friends advised on Jay's progress, slow though it was. Jay never spoke, but he did hum. After hearing a song he liked, even if only once and even if it was a complicated piece, he was able to hum it perfectly from then on. He so loved music.

Hoping to build on this interest, his parents bought a piano and hired a teacher for him. Jay did take the lessons, but lost interest after a while. It's likely that his love of music remained, but it was the *way* he was being taught that didn't work. People with autism learn in ways that are different from the norm, and teachers need special training to be effective.

Water was something else that attracted Jay, and they had a large shallow end in their pool for him. He spent most of each day in the pool, gliding through the water gracefully. "Like a porpoise," Lloyd would say. This form of physical therapy seemed to even out Jay's moods that, otherwise, would often be volatile and difficult to control.

☆☆☆

While Lloyd's stock had dropped a little since the beginning of the decade, he still was a recognizable name. As the second half of the twentieth century began, Lloyd began to explore new avenues to ply his trade. This journey would lead to the most professionally rewarding phase of his life.

CHAPTER 11

Who Needs Movies When You Have Television and the Stage

Between 1950 and 1953, Lloyd only made one feature. It was Bob Hope's *The Lemon Drop Kid,* based on a Damon Runyon story. The film was shot in 1950, but the release was held up until April of 1951. It was a strange decision by Paramount as the film was set around Christmas time. (Hollywood always had a bad sense of timing. Another mistimed release, the Christmas classic, *Miracle on 34*th *Street,* was released in May of 1947.) In this Sidney Lanfield (with Frank Tashlin uncredited) tale, Lloyd plays a Runyanesque gangster, Oxford Charlie. Marilyn Maxwell is the female interest. The film is sprinkled with other Runyon people with names like Moose Moran (Fred Clark), Straight Flush (Jay C. Flippen), and Gloomy Willie (William Frawley). The film is best known for introducing the Jay Livingston and Ray Evans Christmas classic "Silver Bells," sung by Bob and Marilyn.

The rest of Lloyd's time was spent performing in the Theatre Guild play *The Silver Whistle* in 1950. This quaint drama, which was produced on the Broadway stage in 1948 and starred Jose Ferrer, was

Lloyd as Oliver Erwenter in *The Silver Whistle*

set in a home for the elderly. The protagonist of the play is Oliver Erwinter, who is, in reality, Wilfred Tassbinder, a tramp who finds a birth certificate that had belonged to a seventy-seven-year-old man. Oliver moves into an old-age home and shows the residents and staff the meaning of their still-active lives. After completing his mission, he moves on. Lloyd played the lead role in a road company. He excelled. Writing in the *Baltimore Sun*, Donald Kirkley exclaimed, "We may be thankful too that Lloyd Nolan has returned from Hollywood to take the leading pivotal role." Kirkley added, "Mr. Nolan aided by a fine speaking voice brings out all phases of the character clearly." At one of his many performances all over the country was Broadway producer Paul Gregory. He would remember Nolan's fine performance.

Lloyd turned to the small screen. His television debut came in 1950 in a live *Ford Television Theater Hour* production of *The Barker*, based on a 1927 Broadway play that starred Walter Huston, Claudette Colbert and Norman Foster. (Miss Colbert and Mr. Foster would marry, following the run of the play.) *The Barker* is the story of a woman who comes between a father and his estranged son. The play would be filmed by Warner Bros. in 1928 as a part-talkie with Milton Sills, Dorothy Mackaill, Betty Compson and Douglas Fairbanks Jr. Fox remade it in 1933 and called it *Hoop-La*, which starred Clara Bow, Preston Foster and Richard Cromwell. Fox did it as a musical called *Billy Rose's Diamond Horseshoe*, with Betty Grable, Dick Haymes and William Gaxton. Lloyd's co-stars in this TV version were Jean Carson, Eileen Heckart (her debut), and William Redfield.

Lloyd was back on the stage in a play called *Courtin' Time*. It was an original story based on the British play *The Farmer's Wife*, by Eden Philpotts. Filmed as a silent in 1928, it was directed by, of all people,

Alfred Hitchcock. The part required Lloyd to sing. He had done some singing earlier in his stage career and, in fact, the *Philadelphia Inquirer* called Lloyd "an able baritone." It added, "It seemed unbelievable that this man could sing so well." Lloyd wasn't ready for this type of strain on his voice. He caught a cold during the tryouts in Boston. By the time it got to Philadelphia, his throat was beginning to hurt. By the time the company got to Philadelphia, the throat forced him to leave the show. Director Alfred Drake took over the part and, when the show hit Broadway in June of 1951, Joe E. Brown had the job. It mattered not; *Courtin' Time* lasted only thirty-seven performances.

In 1951, Lloyd was named "the best-dressed detective in TV" by the manufacturers of clothing. He was presented with a carnation by beautiful Liza Loughlin.

Back at home, seven-year-old Jay was still non-verbal, and he now had some other disconcerting behaviors, as well. After doing some research, their physician referred the Nolans to a doctor who was known worldwide for his expertise in children with Jay's symptoms. When they arrived in the doctor's office, however, they were very disappointed to learn that there had been a scheduling conflict, and they had to meet with his assistant instead. Upon returning home, they complained to their referring doctor about this outcome. He confided to them that he was hoping they would be able to meet with the assistant because he felt he was a better doctor than the other. Protocol, however, had kept him from making the appointment directly with the assistant, whose name just happened to be Dr. Benjamin Spock.

Spock's diagnosis? "[Jay] is probably brilliant but he won't let you know it." They then learned that Jay's condition had a name: infantile autism.

It was a frustrating situation because autism was not as recognized or understood back then as it is now. Nevertheless, Mell and Lloyd loved Jay dearly, just as they did Melinda.

☆☆☆

While Lloyd was in New York, he was offered the starring role in the television series *Martin Kane, Private Eye*. The show began on radio back in 1947 with William Gargan in the title role. The show was sponsored by the United States Tobacco Company and a plot device that was used throughout the radio and television series had Kane stopping at the local tobacco shop owned by Happy McMann (played wonderfully by Walter Kinsella) to talk about the case he was working on. Inevitably, a customer came in to the shop, giving Happy

a chance to extol the virtues of United States Tobacco Company products. Lloyd would replace Gargan for the series' third season, 1951-52,
and Lee Tracy would replace Lloyd when the series started the fourth
season. Each of the three stars did radio duty as well as television. The
TV shows were done live, thus the turnover in the leading character
as first Gargan and then Lloyd had movie conflicts. Lloyd didn't particularly enjoy this series, but at least it was a regular paycheck. It was
quite a nice paycheck for the time, in fact--$250,000 per year. That was
quite an improvement over the $50,000 per film for three films per
year that he received when working in B movies. He felt that the show
wasn't done well, however, and its director was bad. Even so, that director had a wife and children to support, so Lloyd didn't want to have
him fired. Another reason he was less than enthusiastic about doing
this show was the fact that, since the show was done in New York and
Lloyd wanted to be near the family, Lloyd commuted back and forth
from Brentwood to the Apple. In these days before jet travel, the trip
took twelve hours; and that had to put a strain on Lloyd.

☆☆☆

Lloyd and Mell would soon be making big money in real estate, as
well. About twenty acres of their ranch would be utilized for the new
Ventura Freeway, and a developer wanted to build on the remaining
acres. Since the man who was taking care of their ranch was moving
out of state, they took the developer up on his offer and traded the
ranch for some of his income property. The Nolans probably came
out ahead on that deal because their new land later became the entrance to a shopping center in Thousand Oaks, California.

According to an article in the *TV News* magazine of April, 1952, entitled "TV Portrait Featuring Lloyd Nolan," he had quite a few interests: golfing, handball, swimming and horseback riding. Most of all, he and Mell just loved square dancing and formed their own group called The Beverly Hillbillies. Little did they know that in the next decade that phrase would be the name of a hit television series! Could the show's creator, Paul Henning, have been aware of – or even involved in – the Nolans' square-dancing group? As for culinary preferences, Lloyd loved Chinese food. He had a pet, too – a boxer named Shansie.

Not all was rainbows, however. Actor Wright King recalls an incident that Lloyd related to him once. It was the day of Melinda's prom and she was bedecked in her beautiful gown. Unfortunately, Jay was in the throes of an autistic tantrum and threw—perhaps accidentally—ink on his sister's dress, ruining it.

☆☆☆

Lloyd was brought back to the big screen in 1953 by John Wayne. The "Duke" was the top box-office draw of the era. He had also become a producer with credits that included *Angel and the Badman* and *The Fighting Kentuckian*, both in which he starred. In 1951, he produced Budd Boetticher's *Bullfighter and the Lady,* a truly great film that never got the credit it deserved because John Ford insisted that he take thirty-six minutes out of it. (When it was restored, it finally got credit for being a masterpiece.) Forming a production company with former RKO producer Robert Fellows, Wayne made a distribution deal with Warner Bros. *Island in the Sky* was the second of these films. It is the story of Dooley, an Army transport pilot (Wayne),

Jane Wyatt and Lloyd on *Ford Television Theatre's*
production, "Protect Her Honor"

whose Corsair aircraft is blown off course and runs out of fuel, so he has to crash land on a frozen lake in an uncharted part of Labrador. An alert goes out to headquarters and all of Dooley's friends set out to find him. Lloyd plays one of those pilots (Stutz). Some of the other pilots are played by James Arness, Andy Devine, and Allyn Joslyn. Wayne's crew was made up of Sean McClory (delivering a great performance), Wally Cassel, Hal Baylor and James Lydon. Walter Abel appeared as the commanding officer whose common sense told him to give up the search, but his heart told him to continue. Ernest K. Gann had written the novel and it was immediately picked up by producer Frank Stillman, who planned to have Richard Widmark star as Dooley. Gann and Seton I Miller would write the screenplay. When Stillman dropped the project, Wayne-Fellows picked it up. Gann became much more involved, writing the screenplay by himself. Since Gann was, at the time, a commercial pilot for Transocean Airlines and a veteran of the Air Transport Command at Presque Island, ME, he served as the film's technical director and piloted a plane for the second unit. William Wellman was chosen to direct. Wellman, who had been a pilot in the Lafayette Flying Corps during World War I and had directed a number of aviation pictures, including the first Academy Award winner *Wings,* was the perfect choice. The film got fair reviews; too much was stressed on histrionics and not enough on the action. The photography by Archie Stout, who cut his teeth shooting Hopalong Cassidy films in Lone Pine, California, used his eye well. The story would be done on the *Lux Radio Theater* later in the year, with Dick Powell as Dooley. After this project was completed, Wayne, Wellman, Stout and Gann would combine their talents to make one of the best aviation films of all time, *The High and the Mighty.* Wayne

Lloyd and Mell with John Wayne at the premiere of *Island in the Sky*

did not use any of his ensemble from *Island in the Sky* on this project. (Wayne wasn't even supposed to appear in this. He just wanted to produce it and have Spencer Tracy play Dan Roman, but Tracy wasn't up to the role.) It is interesting to speculate as to what Lloyd could have done as one of the passengers.

Instead, Lloyd went back to the gridiron for the biopic *Crazylegs*, the story of Elroy "Crazylegs" Hirsch. Hirsch played himself; Lloyd played Win "Brock" Brockmeyer, Hirsch's high-school football coach and narrator of the film. The movie follows Hirsch's football career from high school, to college at the University of Wisconsin, to NFL player for the Los Angeles Rams. Hall Bartlett produced this film and Hirsch, who had never acted before, did a competent job. He would act in two more Bartlett films, the underrated *Unchained* and *Zero Hour* (the film that would be spoofed in the hilarious *Airplane!*).

Around this time the United Jewish Appeal was on a campaign to promote the six-year-old state of Israel and raise money for their charity. They went to Hollywood and producers obliged. The first project was a short called *The Great Moment,* and it starred Robert Young, Donna Reed, and John Derek. They followed this up with *Man on a Bus,* which starred Broderick Crawford, Ruth Roman and J. Carrol Naish. The UJA then approached Lloyd and his co-star of yore, Lynn Bari, to narrate a documentary about Israel in 1954. "Both Bari and Nolan donated their salaries for this project to an Israeli charity," wrote Jeff Gordon in his Lynn Bari biography, *Foxy Lady.*

Lloyd's return to movies should have signaled a rebirth of his film career, but an offer was coming up that would define his career.

CHAPTER 12
You Fight the War

Herman Wouk completed *The Caine Mutiny* in 1951. Much of it was taken from actual incidences that took place while he served aboard a dilapidated World War I minesweeper called the *Zane,* and was later transferred to another minesweeper called the *Southard.* At the end of the war, Wouk was an executive officer of the *Southard,* with a recommendation to relieve the captain, but the ship was swamped in a typhoon before he could take over. The mutiny itself was fictional as there has never been a mutiny in the history of the United States Navy, something noted in the prologue of the 1954 film. The book was written entirely through the eyes of Willie Keith, an ensign on the *Caine.*

The book was a smashing success. Movie producer Stanley Kramer purchased the rights just after the book came out. Kramer had produced several controversial films, including *Home of the Brave,* one of the first films to take on racial prejudices. He was putting the finishing touches on *High Noon* when he opted for the Wouk novel, which told the story of a fictional mutiny aboard the *USS Caine,* a battle-weary minesweeper captained by a battle-weary Captain Queeg, who has shown signs of fatigue. When Queeg appears to panic during a typhoon, the executive officer, Steve Maryk, relieves the captain under article 184 of the US Naval regulations. Maryk and Keith are tried for mutiny and they are defended by attorney Barney Greenwald, who gets them off by proving Queeg had been under too much strain. At the end, it is revealed that the whole incident was a plot instigated by Communications Officer Tom Keefer, a disgruntled author who is writing a novel proving the Navy's incompetence.

Prior to the production of the film, Wouk reworked the book into a two-act play focusing on the court-martial. The construction of the play was quite different than the story and the film. While Willie Keith was the pseudo-narrator of the book and the Queeg-Maryk conflict headed the film, defense attorney Barney Greenwald was star of the play. (In the film and the book, Greenwald didn't appear until two thirds into the story.) Lloyd was chosen to play Captain Queeg. When the play's producer, Paul Gregory, was asked on the radio program *Silver Screen Audio* what prompted him to place Lloyd in the role, he was very definitive in his answer: "On stage you don't have the time to establish the circumstances of a character. Lloyd had an intensity of desperation that I liked and I felt the part should have that. Queeg is only on once and his impression had to be immense. Actors who could come out and act is one thing, but actors who can embody that kind of urgency is something else. I felt that Lloyd was ideal and fought to get him." Gregory went on, "It was a hurt that Lloyd had, a subconscious hurt, something that he wasn't even aware that it came through. I had seen him perform before and there was a quality of sadness to Lloyd that was wonderful. I just loved the man."

Lloyd's co-stars, Henry Fonda as Greenwald, John Hodiak as Maryk, and Robert Gist as Keefer, were excellent, as well, in their roles, but Fonda gave producer Gregory and director Charles Laugh-

Candid of Lloyd, Tyrone Power, Raymond Massey, John Hodiak, director
Charles Laughton, unidentified player, Dick Powell, and Henry Fonda

ton problems. Remembers Gregory, "I don't care if Henry Fonda was
the biggest box office in the world. He was the craziest, unpredictable,
unresponsible, irresponsible horror that I ever knew and I had him
thirty weeks in the show. It almost killed me." Lloyd remembered an
incident which verified Fonda's unprofessional behavior. In a 1962 article by Hedda Hopper, Lloyd remembered Fonda getting disturbed
by off-stage noises during a performance. "He gets very intense," said
Lloyd. "I remember there was a squeaky chair and some hapless stage
hand sat on it. We had come off, and were ready to take our bow when
Henry grabbed it, threw it against the wall and stepped on it, smashing
it to pieces. The curtain was up and they were waiting for us to come
out again but he wouldn't come out until he'd destroyed the chair."

Capt. Queeg (Lloyd) reads fitness report on Lt. Steve Maryk
during scene from *The Caine Mutiny Court Martial*. Lt. Barney
Greenwald (Henry Fonda) is cross-examining attorney.

It is rare that a play and a film run at the same time. The film that starred Humphrey Bogart as Queeg, Van Johnson as Maryk, Jose Ferrer as Greenwald, Robert Francis as Keith and Fred MacMurray as Keefer, opened in September of 1954, nine months after the play opened. It is even more rare that two events could be the same, yet so different.

Lloyd stole the show with his Queeg. Paul Gregory's instinct was spot on. Lloyd's Queeg showed a sensitivity and intensity that made the theatergoer feel sorry for him, something that Bogart was not able to establish in the film because many of the incidents that led to the mutiny were visible to the viewer. This Pulitzer Prize-winning play would bring Lloyd much praise; critic Brooks Atkinson was mightily impressed. He wrote, "Nolan's portrait of fear, desperation and panic is a stunning piece of work." Walter Kerr, another respected drama critic, added that, even though Lloyd's "character is wildly out of control, the actor continues to shape—and make meaningful—all his exhausting effects." He saw none of Nolan's previous characters in this one.

Lloyd won the Donaldson and the New York Drama Critics' Award as the outstanding Broadway actor of the 1953-54 season, as well as the Disabled Veterans Art Guild's award as the most outstanding actor on the Broadway stage in the 1953-54 season.

Knowing how to best manage his time for ultimate performance in a stage play, Nolan would come backstage after the first scene and take a nap until the stage manager woke him up five minutes before his cue. He was now refreshed and ready for the long, demanding second-act scene. As Hal Erickson, in his *All Movie Guide*, said, "Nolan originated the role of the paranoid Captain Queeg in the Broadway play *The Caine Mutiny Court Martial*, wherein he'd emerge from a

THEATRE ARTS

50 CENTS

April 1954 • Special Section: "The Plight of the Living Theatre in the United States" by O. Glenn Saxon, Professor of Economics, Yale University • Complete Play: "Picnic" by William Inge

John Hodiak, Henry Fonda and Lloyd Nolan in Broadway season's big hit, "The Caine Mutiny Court Martial" pleasant backstage nap to play some of the most gut-wrenching 'character deterioration' scenes ever written."

Other than Lloyd's scene as Captain Queeg, the other highlight was Barney Greenwald's final speech to Maryk and Keith. Both Wouk's novel and play hinted at anti-Semitism on the part of the Navy. When Greenwald is introduced at the court martial, the judge advocate refers to him as "That Jewish Fellow." When Greenwald gets the *Caine* officers acquitted, he goes out and gets drunk. At a party after the trial, he confronts the officers and reveals Keefer's plot to write his book and embarrass the Navy. Greenwald tells the men that he got them off by torpedoing Queeg and hated himself for doing it because "When Hitler came to power, he hated Jews; he said that they were vermin. They should be melted down into soap. Who was watching over poor Mrs. Greenwald? Queeg and a lot of men like him, men that didn't crack up under pressure. I shot down Queeg and I'm sick about it. Queeg kept Hitler from washing his hands with my mother." Maryk then understands that they *are* guilty. He questions Greenwald, asking him, "What do you do when faced with a Captain who is not up to standards that you set?" Greenwald's reply: "You fight the war." This whole component was avoided in the film version, though it was part of the book. Why Kramer, who was himself was both Jewish and an advocate of civil rights, eliminated this is a question that may never be answered.

The Caine Mutiny Court Martial ran from January 20, 1954 to January 22, 1955, a total of four hundred fifteen performances, at the Plymouth Theatre. After Fonda left the cast to film *Mister Roberts,* where he got into a fight with John Ford and had him replaced with Mervyn LeRoy, Barry Sullivan replaced him and told *TV Guide* reporter Rob-

PROGRAMS · PEOPLE · WEEK OF NOV. 13-19

New York Herald Tribune
SECTION 9

TV and *Radio* *Magazine*

LLOYD NOLAN'S
CAPT. QUEEG
COMES TO TV

Bringing Broadway to television

ert de Roos, "I thought I knew a lot about acting, but Lloyd's so enormously good you can't help absorbing something from his work. He turned in one of the two or three greatest performances of the American theater."

It was Sullivan who played Greenwald in the 1955 television version, the only visible evidence of Lloyd's brilliant performance. Frank Lovejoy played Maryk, replacing Hodiak, who had just passed away at the age of forty-one. Gist, soon to become an accomplished television director, repeated his role as Keefer. Lloyd won an Emmy for his performance. "We both were nominated for the Emmy," Barry Sullivan said, "and I voted for him. I'll bet Lloyd was a unanimous choice." It is interesting that *The Caine Mutiny* was never remade, but *The Caine Mutiny Court Martial* was revived several times. The first was in 1983 at the Circle in the Square with John Rubinstein, Michael Moriarty and Jay O. Saunders as Maryk. He would be replaced by former National Football League quarterback Joe Namath. A year later, Charlton Heston played Queeg in a London production, to much critical acclaim. He later brought it to the Kennedy Center in Washington, DC, to the same reaction. Robert Altman filmed the *Caine Mutiny Court Martial* in 1988 with Eric Bogosian, Jeff Daniels and Brad Davis as Queeg. Despite the various portrayals, it is unanimously agreed that Lloyd Nolan *was* Captain Queeg.

☆☆☆

Until now, Lloyd and his friend Fred MacMurray had owned the apartments at 426-428 South Spalding Drive in Beverly Hills. The twelve-unit building also had a heated swimming pool, cabanas, sub-

Lloyd with his Emmy in one hand and his famous prop in the other.
The award, for "best actor in a single performance," was presented
to him by William Holden at the 8th annual awards ceremony
on March 19, 1956. (Courtesy of Bettmann/Corbis Images)

terranean garage, and a recreation area. They sold it in March, 1955, to Otto Hinsche. He also did some investing: in a frozen food plant and an apartment house. In a January, 1957, *New York Post* column, Sidney Skolsky acknowledged that Lloyd was an astute businessman. Lloyd agreed. "I might have been a stock broker," he remarked, "if I hadn't decided to become an actor."

Back in Hollywood in 1956, Lloyd went to MGM to make another western, *The Last Hunt*. He had the showy role of Woodfoot, a peg-legged alcoholic who, at one time, was the best mule skinner in the territory. He joins a Buffalo hunt led by Charlie Gilson, a sadistic violent man (Robert Taylor, in a great performance) and Sandy McKenzie (Stewart Granger). Russ Tamblyn and Debra Paget complete the group. Charlie eventually goes insane, kills Woodfoot, and looks to finish off the rest of the party. The final scene is a memorable one as director Richard Brooks pulls no punches. Looking at Lloyd in *The Last Hunt,* it is hard to recognize him until he speaks. Renowned Hollywood columnist Joe Hyams had scheduled an interview with Lloyd while he was filming the western. On the set, he came across a bearded old wreck sitting on a cap chair, whittling. Hyams asked him if he had seen Lloyd. The reply was, "Sit down, son, he'll be right with you." The old man finished his whittling, folded up his jackknife, smiled and said, "He's here." Hyams had been taken by the immense set of whiskers and shabby clothes.

Lloyd enjoyed the scene-stealing part of Woodfoot. He explained to Hyams how he was able to portray a man walking with a stump:

A very different "look" in *The Last Hunt*

"I have a gimmick which straps my foot back at the knee for any angle required for the shots. In long shots of me, a double with a real wooden leg is used. Most of the close-ups are from the waist up." The beard that Lloyd used was real. "It's a lot easier to grow your own than to sit in a makeup chair for an hour while they glue it on and for another when they take it off."

Hyams wasn't the only one fooled. "The other day I passed Paul Gregory in a hotel lobby," Lloyd told Hyams. "He was talking with Agnes Moorehead. I was going up to say hello when I heard Paul say to Agnes, 'look at that old character.'"

It had been nearly a decade since Lloyd played a real villain. Why he chose *Santiago* more than likely was for the pay day and a chance to work again with Alan Ladd, with whom he clicked nine years earlier in *Wild Harvest*. Ladd and Lloyd play rival gun runners who are also

With Alan Ladd in *Santiago*

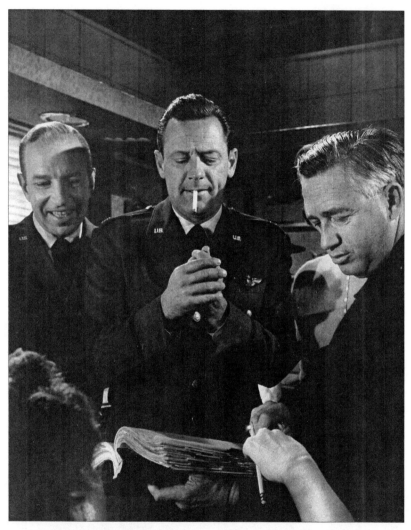

Lloyd, William Holden, and director Mervyn LeRoy, checking
script details with script supervisor Dorothy Aldrin, prior to
filming a scene of T*oward the Unknown*

competing for the hand of Rosanna Podesta. Had this film been made ten years earlier, it might have been better, but Ladd had not aged well and seemed to have lost much of his appeal, while Lloyd, at fifty-four years, was too old to play this character. Ladd eventually wins Podesta, but it was hardly a point of emphasis in the resumes of all concerned.

Lloyd's final film of 1956 was much better. It was *Toward the Unknown.* Lloyd was very believable as General Bill Banner in a film that starred William Holden as Major Lincoln Bond, once a hotshot pilot who was captured and tortured during the Korean War. Bond comes to Edwards Air Force Base, hoping to get a job as a test pilot. General Banner, the commanding officer, has to refuse but, after Banner cracks up and is rescued by Bond, Banner gives him a chance.

Bond redeems himself, gets his confidence back in this literate film written by Beirne Lay, Jr. (who co-wrote the Oscar-winning *Twelve O'Clock High*) and directed by Mervyn LeRoy. Holden's production company, Toluca Productions, financed the film. Lloyd enjoyed working with Holden.

Marie Torre wrote in her February 9, 1956, column in the *New York Herald Tribune* that Lloyd would go to Hollywood to film a TV pilot, *Father Duffy of Hell's Kitchen.* The show, based on the real-life Father Francis Patrick Duffy, a World War I hero, inspired international admiration for his valiant efforts as chaplain of the Fighting 69th during the dark hours in France. (Father Duffy was portrayed by Pat O'Brien in Warner Bros.' *The Fighting 69th.*) While the pilot was supposed to be filmed in early August for Desilu Productions, it never got off the ground.

So Lloyd stayed in London, not only performing *The Caine Mutiny Court Martial* at the London Hippodrome, but serving as director as well. Co-starring with him in this production were David Knight,

**Doing research for the Father Duffy role,
Lloyd showed Mell an item of interest**

Esmond Knight, and Nigel Stock. Producing were Henry Sherek and
Gilbert Miller. The London production ran for twenty weeks.

His role in this play had totaled two years now and six-hundred-
eighteen performances. Within a couple of days after the final curtain
call, however, he had forgotten every one of his lines. Lloyd could
memorize his lines and perform them to perfection in the play, but in
all other areas of his life, he had a notoriously poor memory.

It was during the London run in 1956 that Lloyd and Mell came
to a difficult decision. They both loved Jay dearly and wanted him to
have the best life possible. Melinda had been very sweet to her young
brother, but it was becoming evident that she preferred going to her
friends' homes, rather than inviting them to hers. Jay's sometimes-vio-
lent behavior would make others uncomfortable and somewhat judg-
mental of the Nolans' parenting abilities. There's no doubt that having
an autistic child puts a huge strain on the family and the marriage. Because their son had never spoken, it was oftentimes difficult to know
what he needed at any given time. Lloyd faced the truth first, and then
convinced Mell, that they should place their son in a special school. In
such a school, Jay would receive the 24/7 care that they were unable to
give him at home. The caretakers there were accustomed to autistic behavior and knew how to handle it. Lloyd and Mell realized what they
had to do and, once back in the States, began to search in earnest for
the best school in which to place him. At the Institute for Achievement
of the Human Potential in Philadelphia, they found what they were
looking for. It was with very mixed feelings—love, agony, hope—that
they moved him into his new home. This, Lloyd felt later, had been
"the end." They would visit Jay very, very often; but living on opposite
coasts took something away from their relationship. No longer would

they see Jay's sweet face every day and tuck him in bed each night. And now Lloyd had a new worry—that he might someday run out of money to take care of Jay. Schools like this are very, very expensive.

Society, in general, was not kind to such developmentally-disabled children in the 1950s, which made raising them even more difficult. Jay was now in the hands of professionals who understood and valued him. That was of some consolation to his parents.

The nurses at Jay's new home discovered something fascinating about him. To them, it sounded like he was just making loud noises. When preschool-aged children were around, however, they were able to tell the nurses what it was that Jay was trying to say. It seemed that he could communicate effectively only with very young children.

★★★

While Lloyd was in the United Kingdom, he had an opportunity to play in one of his most underrated films, *Abandon Ship,* released in 1957. Co-starring with his *Johnny Apollo* buddy, Tyrone Power, who was also appearing on the West End, starring in *The Devil's Disciple,* this film is an excellent rendering of a story supposedly based on fact (though a story in the *New York Times* casts doubt about the validity of the claim) of a ship that sinks in the Atlantic after striking an abandoned land mine. Of the 1,256 passengers, only twenty-seven survive. Power plays the ship's executive officer, Alex Holmes, who is thrust into the position of having to rule over the twenty-seven clinging onto a lifeboat that can only hold nine. In order to save some of the survivors, Holmes has to order some of the excess personage to their sure deaths. Lloyd plays Frank Kelly, the ship's engineer, who is injured in the explosion and who is the first to voluntarily give up his life to save others. Richard Sale directed this claustrophobic tale in the spirit of Alfred Hitchcock's *Lifeboat* (1944). Sale's camera movement is much more fluid than Hitchcock's, who concentrated more on character development and pontificating in *Lifeboat*. *Abandon Ship* focuses more on the story. Both films do their job well. This was Power's only film appearance for his Copa Productions.

Whether Lloyd was in Egypt in 1956 because of the play or some other reason is unknown, but that's where and when his lifelong passion for archaeology began. This keen interest meshed well with his other avid hobby, traveling. It was also in this year that he and Mell began their yearly extended pilgrimage to Europe. They would often stay a month, sometimes making the trip twice in a year. The couple found something memorable everywhere they went—their favorite cuisine could be found in Italy; they had a fender-bender in Yugoslavia and got off easy because the woman judge had seen Lloyd on screen, and the Nolans both adored Greece.

Recalls Don Lightfoot:

> Whenever Lloyd and Mell traveled to another country, they always came back with stories of people they met. Some were very famous or politically powerful, but the ones they really were impressed with were the people they met on sightseeing tours or kids on the street. In Spain, they met a young man who offered to do errands for them. They kept in touch with him and made sure his education was paid for. A guide assigned to them during a visit to Russia became a friend and, even through the difficulties of political

(Cold War) censorship, they were able to financially participate in her wedding. They loved to help anyone that they knew needed a helping hand.

Lloyd was now being paid $50,000 per film and was appearing in three pictures a year. His next 1957 film was another of his underappreciated performances, appearing as John Pope, Sr. in the brilliant *A Hatful of Rain*. Adapted from the play which starred Ben Gazzara, Shelley Winters, Frank Silvera and Anthony Franciosa, director Fred Zinnemann used actual New York City locations to enhance the brilliant acting by the film leads.

Johnny Pope (Don Murray) has become an addict, a fact unknown to his wife Celia (Eva Marie Saint) and his father John, Sr. (Lloyd). Only Johnny's brother, Polo (Anthony Franciosa, recreating his Broadway role), knows about it and works as a bouncer in a club

With Don Murray, Anthony Franciosa, and Eva Marie Saint in *A Hatful of Rain*

to finance his habit. John, Sr. comes from his home in Florida to New York to get money that Polo has put aside for him to open a bar. In John, Sr.'s eyes, Johnny has been the golden boy and Polo has been the failure. As Johnny tries to fight the addiction long enough to get his father to return to Florida, things unravel for him. He and Celia realize he has a massive problem that needs attention.

The final scene in this movie is one of the great closers ever filmed, with Celia calling the police, reporting Johnny as an addict and, answering the question who the addict is, cries, "*It's my husband.*" It's a remarkable piece of acting.

Lloyd should have gotten an Oscar nomination for this one, but Fox was pushing the younger Franciosa, who lost to Alec Guinness for *The Bridge on the River Kwai*. Lloyd's John Pope, Sr. is a wonderful interpretation of a father plagued by personal failure (at his age, he's still tending bar), frustration (he quit his job to open his own place, but the money Polo promised him was spent on Johnny), and guilt (his inability to provide a home for the brothers when their mother died, thus they had to be placed in an orphanage). He can't accept the fact that his son Johnny has sunk so low and that he is in real trouble. It is a masterpiece, a challenge along the lines of Captain Queeg.

Don Murray remembers the making of that motion picture very clearly. "*A Hatful of Rain* was one of the most rewarding creative experiences of my life," he says. "If one considers all of Fred Zinnemann's films, he has to be recognized as one of the all-time great directors. The atmosphere on the set was perfect; dedicated, serious, but not grim—totally enjoyable. What impressed my experience with Lloyd Nolan the most was that he was from the era of movies where stars were 'personalities' first and it often seemed that their main aim was to get out as many words in as short a time as possible. Eva Marie, Tony Franciosa and I are from the 'reality' school of acting. Lloyd wielded with that reality perfectly. He seemed to genuinely feel the emotions of the character, just as we did. There was no sense of an actor with him. He was my father and stirred the emotions of our relationship in a way that was felt as genuine." Murray concluded, "He deserves to be considered one of the finest actors, not only of his time, but of all time."

Lloyd, too, had tremendous respect for director Zinnemann. In a 1976 interview with Richard Fernandez, he put Zinnemann on the highest pedestal. "Of all of the directors I worked with, Fred Zinnemann stands alone. Henry Hathaway, whom I worked with on several pictures, was a good director but a son-of-a bitch once he got on the set. Tay Garnett was a simple and easy man to work with."

Besides the leads, *A Hatful of Rain* benefited from great performances from the supporting cast, especially Henry Silva, who also was imported from the Broadway cast. In addition, Bernard Herrmann composed one of the best scores of his career.

Besides an Oscar nomination for Franciosa, Zinnemann was nominated for a DGA award; Eva Marie Saint, Zinnemann and Franciosa were nominated for Golden Globes. This was the year for *The Bridge on the River Kwai* and *Peyton Place,* so the nominations were the best recognition the film would receive.

In an era that would produce other films about drug addiction, Otto Preminger's *The Man with the Golden Arm* and the biopic of boxer Barney Ross, *Monkey on My Back,* the film that stands above the others is *A Hatful of Rain.*

Grace Metalious wrote *Peyton Place* in 1956. Her novel told of things like incest, abortion, rape, adultery and murder. The town of

Peyton Place was believed to have been Gilmanton, New Hampshire, but many believe that other towns could have been identified as Peyton Place. Several of the characters in the book were real-life characters that Metalious knew. The book sold sixty thousand copies the first ten days it was released. Word of mouth spread like wildfire, and the book became the second-biggest blockbuster of all time (*Gone with the Wind* was the top). It stayed on the *New York Times* bestseller list for fifty-nine weeks. In late 1956, 20th Century-Fox purchased the rights to the book for $100,000. Other studios were not interested in the book as it was deemed unfilmable. John Michael Hayes was given the job of carving out a screenplay, which would be toned down due to the Production Code, which eliminated many of unacceptable elements of the book.

Hope Lange and Lloyd in *Peyton Place*

On the back of this framed photo is written, "Left to right: Senator (then) Kennedy, Mark Robson (director), Sen. Edmund Muskie, Lloyd Nolan, Lee Philips (actor), and Congressman (who?). On location for 'Peyton Place' in Camden, Maine (Early '50s)." (From the collection of Nolan Lightfoot)

The film tells the story of Constance MacKenzie (Lana Turner), owner of a dress shop, her illegitimate daughter, Allison (Diane Varsi), who is an aspiring writer, and her friend from the wrong side of the tracks, Selena Cross (Hope Lange). There are many other characters in the story. The new school principal, Michael Rossi (Lee Philips), who falls in love with Constance, Betty Anderson (Terry Moore), the town tramp in love with Rodney Harrington (Dick Davalos), son of the town's leading employer and richest man, Norman Paige (Russ Tamblyn), a sensitive boy dominated by his possessive mother, and Lucas Cross (Arthur Kennedy in a brave performance), one of the most deplorable characters ever portrayed on a screen. Lloyd plays Dr Matthew Swain, the town doctor and the voice of reason in a scandal- and gossip-filled village.

Many of the exterior scenes were filmed in various parts of Maine and New Hampshire, adding realism to the film. Fred Perkins, the continuity director at a local Maine radio station, served as dialectician on the film.

The film was nominated for many awards. Once again, Lloyd was ignored. Lana Turner was nominated for best actress (Joanne Wood ward won for *The Three Faces of Eve*), Arthur Kennedy and Russ Tamblyn were nominated for best Supporting Actor (Red Buttons won for *Sayonara*), Hope Lange and Diane Varsi both got Supporting Actress nods (Miyoshi Umeki won for *Sayonara),* and Mark Robson was nominated for Best Director (won by David Lean for *Kwai*).

The highest accolade of all was for Lloyd when *Peyton Place* author Grace Metalious felt that of all the players in that film, Lloyd was the only one whose performance was worthy of her praise.

1957 was a bounce back for Lloyd, but it would be three years before he would return to the Big Screen, and once again Lana Turner would appear with him.

CHAPTER 13

More Opportunities on the Tube

The year 1958 brought a pleasant surprise. On June 9, the Pasadena Playhouse presented Lloyd with a Master's Degree. Participating in the ceremony were Gilmore Brown, who was President and founder of the Playhouse, and actor Robert Young.

While Lloyd was off the screen for two years, he was far from being inactive. Television was growing up, and there were three basic components to the adolescent period of the medium. You had the young, talented actor on the way up. Several, like Clint Eastwood (*Rawhide*), Steve McQueen (*Wanted: Dead or Alive*), and James Garner (*Maverick*), went on to become major stars. Others, like James Arness (*Gunsmoke*), Raymond Burr (*Perry Mason*), Robert Stack (*The Untouchables*), and Lucille Ball (*I Love Lucy*) reached a pinnacle in television that they could never surpass, should they return full time to the big screen. The third was the former leading man who was given a series of his own or "guest-starring" roles on other series, like Edmond O'Brien (*Johnny Midnight, Sam Benedict*), Broderick Crawford (*Highway Patrol*), and Craig Stevens (*Peter Gunn*).

Lloyd had joined a fine cast that included Victor Jory, Martha Vickers and James Whitmore in a *Playhouse 90* episode called "The Galvanizing Yankee," then accepted an offer to do a television show of his own called *Special Agent 7*. The deal was struck with his agents, MCA, and the show was produced by a company called Television Programs of America (TPA). TPA, formed by successful independent producer Edward Small, whose credits included great *noirs* like *T-Men, Scandal Sheet,* and *Kansas City Confidential,* Leon Fromkess, who had headed Poverty Row studio PRC, and, Chicago lawyer Milton Gordon. TPA had had a history of producing successful syndicated shows, using many of Lloyd's old screen cronies, like Buster Crabbe (*Captain Gallant of the Foreign Legion*), J. Carrol Naish (*The New Adventures of Charlie Chan*), and Lee Tracy (*New York Confidential*). Another co-star of Lloyd's was also involved in a TPA series, and that was Lassie (through a partnership with the Collie's producer Jack Wrather). Lloyd was convinced that *Secret Agent 7* could be an entrance to the television world. Television had changed since Lloyd had done *Martin Kane*. Most shows were now filmed in Hollywood, and Lloyd would have to worry about commuting from coast to coast. The original deal was for twenty-six episodes. Lloyd played an undercover agent, Phillip Conroy, who each week hunts down criminals. At age fifty-seven, Lloyd wasn't ready for the grind of weekly television. After doing twenty-six episodes of the show, he'd had had enough. He threatened to bring suit against MCA. They relented and the show ended. It is too bad that Lloyd had not heard of a concept created by independent producer Don Fedderson, who hired Fred MacMurray to star in a sitcom called *My Three Sons*. Fedderson's concept was to write the episodes for the entire season, then film MacMurray's parts in a three-month span, thus guaranteeing him a year's work with nine months off. The idea worked for twelve years. It is not known if Lloyd's show could have been done that way, and more to the point, *Special Agent 7* was not exactly a high-quality show.

☆☆☆

As the decade came to a close, Melinda was sometimes alone in the house when her parents traveled. She had a job, so couldn't always get time off to accompany them. Not wanting her to be lonely, her parents then asked housekeeper Edna to come stay with her during those times. Even though Edna was about eighty years old, she was still a stern taskmaster. Melinda's boyfriend, Don Lightfoot, knew that he could stay for only a while because Edna had a set time at which he must leave.

Once Edna's physical limitations made it difficult for her to fulfill her housekeeping duties, her daughter Florence took her place. Florence would clean the Nolans' home twice a week for nearly twenty years. Says Don:

> Each time that Florence left for the day, Mell would find a dust cloth left in one of the rooms. This greatly disturbed Mell, but she did not mention it for many years. Finally, she told Florence, and Florence laughed and said she didn't realize that she did that. She didn't do it again until her last day there. She left a dust rag on the table in the hallway. I always felt it was her private little joke.

Meanwhile, Lloyd got a prestige assignment playing Nat Miller, the newspaper publisher and patriarch of the Miller family, in a live *Hall-*

mark *Hall of Fame* presentation of Eugene O'Neill's *Ah, Wilderness!* The play, set in a Connecticut town in 1906, tells the story of young Richard Miller and his coming of age. The play, which opened on Broadway in 1933 and ran for two-hundred-eighty-nine performances, originally starred George M. Cohan, Elisha Cook Jr., and Gene Lockhart. The same year Will Rogers played in a San Francisco company presentation of the play and was requested to play in the movie version made in 1935. He backed out of the assignment. Had he not, he would not have been on the fatal flight that took his and pilot Wiley Post's life that year. Lionel Barrymore took the role of Nat. Lloyd played opposite Helen Hayes, who played his wife Essie, and Betty Field, his sister Lilly. Burgess Meredith and Norman Fell were in the cast as well. An unknown young man from the Actors Studio, Lee Kinsolving, took the key role of the son Arthur and acquitted himself very well. Kinsolving was on his way in the movie business after a sensitive performance in *The Dark at the Top of the Stairs.* All of a sudden he retired from films, being frustrated with show business. He died at the age of thirty-six. *Ah, Wilderness!* was a rare instance where Lloyd did not get great notices. *The New York Times* noted that "Lloyd did not bring too much emotional variation to the part." Unfortunately, this was one of those situations in which live television failed the entire production. The emotional facts-of-life scene between Lloyd and Lee Kinsolving was marred by transmission difficulties, taking the emotion out of the scene.

In 1959, Lloyd hired a new agent, Bill Robinson. For ten years, no contract was signed since they trusted each other completely.

Lloyd then looked to the live stage, from whence he had come. In a life of good decisions, this was not one.

CHAPTER 14

One More River Too Many

One More River was an English play written by Beverley Cross, a London-born author and playwright who was educated at the Nautical Institute at Pangborn. He found inspiration about this, his first form, his pre-Oxford experience, as an ordinary seaman aboard a Norwegian freighter. It was produced on London's West End by Laurence Olivier with great success and was purchased sight unseen by Mary K. Frank.

The play, boasting a fine cast headed by Lloyd and including Alfred Ryder, Harry Guardino, and Al Lewis, was set aboard a tramp freighter in West Africa. The captain has died and the First Mate Sewell (Ryder) is a martinet. Consequently, the crew detests him. Only old man Johnny Condell, the Bos'n (Lloyd), stands up for him, and it leads to him becoming a victim. The role was some sort of irony for Lloyd, as this time he is the character trying to prevent a mutiny, rather than being the victim of one as he was in *The Caine Mutiny Court Martial.* Lloyd was praised for his performance. Whitney Bolton, writing in the *Morning Telegraph*, remarked, "Lloyd Nolan returns to Broadway after an absence of six years, gives his usual expert performance and in two major scenes manages spectacular strength." Robert Coleman, writing in the *New York Daily Mirror*, said Lloyd is "excellent as the efficient and humane Bosun." John Chapman in the *New York Daily News*, wrote, "Nolan is a splendid old sea dog. With perfect ease he can take command of a theatrical audience or a ship manned by a rebellious crew." Ryder, as the captain, garnered excellent reviews as well.

But the play itself was a major problem. The final act was anticlimactic and weak and, in the end, it sunk the play.

One More River opened on March 18, 1960, and closed March 19, 1960. It played for a total of three performances. For Lloyd Nolan, who rose to fame on the Broadway stage, it was hardly the way he wanted his swan song to be chronicled.

Prior to preparation for *One More River,* Lloyd would work on the project that would mark his return to the screen, reuniting him with Lana Turner, his co-star from *Peyton Place.*

Portrait in Black was not a new property. Written in 1945, the play was written by Ivan Goff and Ben Roberts, who would pen Cagney classics like *White Heat* and *Come Fill the Cup* and would create television's *Charlie's Angels.* They sold the property for filming to Universal with a proviso that production would start by June 30, 1950. Meanwhile, the play was produced on the London stage with Diana Wynyard starring. Ms. Wynyard was married at the time to director Carol Reed who wanted to make the film, but backed out due to a disagreement with Universal over the adaptation. Goff and Roberts got the property back, then learned that director Michael Gordon and Joan Crawford were interested in making the film.

The property lay dormant until producer Ross Hunter showed interest. Hunter was the hot young producer who had reshaped Universal Studio's face in the 1950s. Prior to that time, Universal had morphed from a Carl Laemmle studio, which gave Irving Thalberg his start and produced classics like *All Quiet on the Western Front,* to a studio that specialized in *Frankenstein, Dracula, The Wolf Man* films, Abbott and Costello comedies and serials like *Flash Gordon.* During this period, Lloyd had made a "B" film there, *Mr. Dynamite.* By the late forties, they had reused the formula so many times the public was getting tired of it. Universal merged with William Goetz's International Pictures and became Universal-International. They brought in independent producers like Mark Hellinger and signed James Stewart to a deal that gave him a share of the profits as opposed to a straight salary. The concept worked, Stewart's *Winchester '73* made a fortune for both and put the studio back on its feet. By the mid-1950s, Hunter was a contract producer. One assignment given him was *Magnificent Obsession,* taken from a Lloyd C. Douglas book made originally by Universal back in 1935, starring Irene Dunne. By pairing young heart-throb Rock Hunter with Oscar-winning actress Jane Wyman, and adding it to the lush directorial style of Douglas Sirk, Hunter created what would become the staple of U-I for the next decade. Films like *All that Heaven Allows* (reuniting Hudson and Ms. Wyman again), *There's Always Tomorrow* (Barbara Stanwyck and Fred MacMurray), and *Imitation of Life* (Lana Turner in a remake of a 1934 Universal film that starred Claudette Colbert) followed. By this time, Hunter had formed his own production company and, besides the weepies, he also created the *Tammy* series and a series of films reinventing Doris Day as the eternal virgin.

In *Portrait in Black,* while not a villain, Lloyd played a rich shipping magnet, Matthew Cobb, who treats his wife Sheila (Lana Turner) roughly. Sheila is having an affair with Dr. David Rivera (Anthony

Quinn). Sheila and the doctor conspire to kill her husband by inject-
ing him with an untraceable air bubble in his hypodermic. Also on
hand are Cathy (Sandra Dee), Matthew's daughter from a previous
marriage, Cathy's boyfriend Blake (John Saxon), Matthew's second-
in-command Howard (Richard Basehart), and the family chauffer
(Ray Walston). All play significant portions in this melodrama.

One of Lloyd's former co-players at Paramount, Anna May
Wong, playing the Cabot's servant Tani, made her final film appearance in this film, accepting the role after an eleven-year absence. Virginia Grey also appeared as Matthew's secretary, Miss Lee.

Though Lloyd played his part entirely in a reclining position, it
was not as easy as it seems. Lloyd related in a U-I press release, "My
shoulders, elbows and heels are already sore and raw. When I go home
at night, I wish I could turn into a horse so I could sleep standing up. I
thought that playing a role like this would be a bed of roses. It is—but
somebody forgot to take out the thorns."

Lloyd had worked in two straight Lana Turner soapers. His characters in *Peyton Place* and *Portrait in Black* could not have been more
different. Here's what film historian Lon and Debra Davis said about it:

> Lloyd Nolan's veracity as an actor is evident when
> comparing his performances in *Peyton Place* (Twen-
> tieth Century-Fox, 1957) and *Portrait in Black* (Uni-
> versal-International, 1960). Although the roles he
> plays (Dr. Matthew Swain in the former, and Mat-
> thew S. Cabot in the latter) are highly disparate, he
> plays both with the complete sense of belief in the
> certainty of the characters.

In *Peyton Place's* stirring courtroom climax, Dr. Swain reveals all, shocking the close-minded residents into reality. It is an incredibly satisfying dénouement, although it would not have been so in the hands of a less-capable actor. Lloyd Nolan is so credible—and the character's words are so logical—the viewer cannot help but see the tragic situation for what it is. Selena Cross is immediately acquitted of murder charges, and is given a warm reception by her fellow citizens. Although a secondary character, Dr. Swain serves as a major catalyst in the story.

By contrast, Lloyd Nolan as the shipping magnate Matthew S. Cabot of *Portrait in Black* is no benevolent voice of reason. He is an ill-tempered man with only a short time to live. Confined to his bed in his San Francisco mansion, he berates his much-younger wife, Sheila (Lana Turner, also the star of *Peyton Place*), whom he rightly suspects of infidelity. In no time, he is murdered by Dr. David Rivera (Anthony Quinn), his physician and his faithless wife's lover. The sympathy of the viewer is meant, apparently, for Lana Turner's character, but she is spoiled, weak, and difficult to like. Lloyd Nolan's character is not especially sympathetic either, but he is hardly one-dimensional. He has earned the affection of his daughter, the respect of his secretary and his servant and has a faithful companion in a Siamese cat named

Roger. Whatever the role, Lloyd Nolan adds credibil-
ity and authority.

Except for Lana Turner, Anthony Quinn, Sandra Dee, and Ray
Walston, none of the actors knew the ending of the film. Even after
the climax was shot, the four participants and the crew that was present were sworn to secrecy. Even though Lloyd was only in seven of
the three-hundred-fifteen scenes (he worked for only three days on
the film), he felt that he had a significant role. It's the power of the
role, not the size, Lloyd pointed out. "In those seven scenes I can de-
liver more impact on an audience than other performers appearing
on the screen for almost ninety minutes."

No money was spared on Lana Turner's appearance in this film.
Stylist Jean Louis was called on to design fourteen gorgeous costumes
for Lana and an equally-glamorous wardrobe for Sandra Dee. In addition, David Webb Jewelers of New York supplied almost two million
dollars worth of diamonds, pearls and emeralds for Ms. Turner.

One of Lloyd's least-known projects was a 1960 film, *Girl of the
Night*. Starring Anne Francis as a sensitive prostitute who was being
manipulated by her pimp-boyfriend (John Kerr), Lloyd's character,
Dr. Mitchell, gave her the therapy she needed to turn her life around.
Says this fine actress, "Lloyd was an absolute angel to work with—a
lovely experience—always a gentleman, and his wife was a super lady."
Part of the reason for its anonymity was the fact that the Catholic
League of Decency questioned the film's subject matter. It was ru-
mored that it would get a "C" for condemned rating, but once viewed
the League changed it to a special rating, as the film did not display any
graphic violence. It did not help the project, Miss Francis or Lloyd.

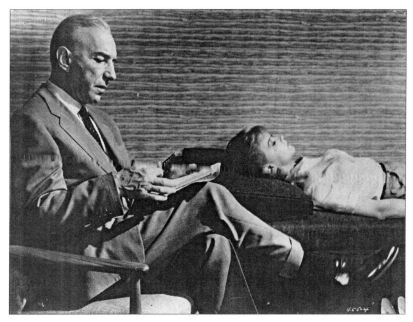

Lloyd played a tough, yet caring, therapist in *Girl of the Night*.
In a scene with Anne Francis.

At this time, Warner Brothers was promoting its television stars to see if a) they could carry a film on the big screen and b) keep them busy during the off season when their respective series were not filming. Such a movie was *Susan Slade,* which starred Connie Stevens and Troy Donahue. Ms. Stevens plays the title role in this soaper with Donahue as her beau (which doesn't happen until the final fadeout). Lloyd plays Roger Slade, a mining engineer returning to the US with daughter Susan and wife Leah (former *A Tree Grows in Brooklyn* co-star Dorothy McGuire) after being on an assignment in Chile for the past ten years. Susan, who has become a woman in that time, embarks on her first affair, with a wealthy mountain climber, Conn White (Grant Williams). Susan becomes pregnant, Conn dies in an accident, Susan keeps the secret from her family, and after a suicide attempt thwarted by a friend, Hoyt (Donahue), it is decided that Roger take a job in Guatemala, where he dies of a heart attack as Leah pretends that she is the mother. They come back to California, where Susan confesses the truth and reunites with Hoyt at the final fadeout.

Connie Stevens tells of the great respect she had for Lloyd. "Mr. Nolan was a consummate professional. Quiet at first and then warm and supportive. I could get him to laugh.... He had the respect of the entire crew and cast. As young as I was at the time, I knew his work and deeply admired him."

It was announced in 1961 that Lloyd had been signed for a top role in an upcoming project titled *Formosa*. The film was to star Rob-

Having a heart attack in the arms of his
daughter (Connie Stevens) in *Susan Slade*

ert Taylor, Lloyd's former co-player from *Bataan*. Taylor had just left MGM after being under contract for almost twenty-five years and was now busy with his television series, *The Detectives*. Robert Fellows would produce the film for Warner Bros. It was to deal with the politically explosive formation of the Island of Formosa. The film was to be shot there, but the project never came to fruition. If the name *Formosa* seems something out of the distant past, it should be. It is now known as Taiwan.

Casting directors knew how highly his peers respected Lloyd, and his integrity was needed for another pilot, entitled *Darrow, the Defender*, about Clarence Darrow, in 1961. Lloyd did his best for them, but, alas, the show failed to sell.

While Lloyd's pilot never got off the runway, his workload, thanks to television, stayed busy. Lloyd guest-starred on many of the popular shows, including *The Untouchables*, where he played the title role in "The George 'Bugs' Moran Story," *Wagon Train*, and *Bonanza*. For Dick Powell, he did two episodes of the *Zane Grey Theater*. He appeared in four episodes of *Laramie* and, when Warner Bros. retooled their famous *77 Sunset Strip* series by creating a multi-part episode called "Five," Lloyd was in each episode. He did not lack for work.

Chuck Southcott, whose stepfather, Andre Dacharry, worked with Lloyd on another project, tells us about this less-than ideal situation: "Andre teamed with Bill Burrud to do a show on the undersea wonders of the islands. The two personalities taken along to be featured were Victor Jory and Lloyd Nolan. I'm told it became a very difficult shoot, since the very liberal Mr. Jory and the very conservative Mr. Nolan fought constantly like the proverbial cats and dogs."

On location, strife was abundant, but at home, love was in the air.

Melinda and Don Lightfoot, who had attended junior high and high school together, were now dating. Says Don:

> Early in my dating Melinda, I recall coming to their home and seeing bright orange spots on their rain gutters. It seems that Lloyd had some free time and decided to touch up some flaking spots. He purchased Rustoleum primer and went wild with it. He then got busy with a movie or some other project and the orange primer stayed a couple of months until Mell called some painters to fix it. Lloyd would always, thereafter, be called "Rusty" by Melinda or her mom when Lloyd started any fix-up work around the house.
>
> I always drove up the long driveway and parked behind the house by the garages. (Brentwood did not like street parking.) One day, Lloyd was looking under the hood of his Jaguar (specially outfitted with Rolls-Royce seats for added comfort) as I drove up. It seemed that a rattle had developed and he thought he would try to find it before he took the car to the mechanic. We started the car and both spotted the loose wing-nut on the air cleaner. Lloyd turned and walked away so I tightened the wing-nut with my fingers. Lloyd came back with a pair of pliers and a crescent wrench. He thanked me for tightening the nut, but had a very sad look of disappointment on his face. I always felt that I had taken away an opportunity, and good feeling, of fixing something from him.

Another time I walked into the backyard and saw Lloyd cutting down a birch tree that was growing too close to the great house. This tree was only about 8" in diameter, but maybe 15 to 20 feet high. His saw would bind up so I went over and leaned against the tree to help keep the saw from binding. Neither of us saw any problem with the fact that he was cutting this tree at ground level until he sawed completely through. We were immediately both holding this tree up, hugging it with our faces about 1" from each other and got the giggles. How dumb could two guys get? We shoved the tree toward the yard and it landed in the pool. Lloyd just walked over to the poolside phone, called the pool guy, and asked him if he could come over the next day to clean out the "leaves" that had fallen into the pool.

Many times, after bringing Melinda home from our date, I would sit with Lloyd and watch TV until about 2:00 a.m. We watched old "B" movies. Lloyd would tell me personal stories about relationships, lifestyles, problems on the set, who didn't like who, etc. Once, after watching a beautiful actress in a very touching love scene, Lloyd commented on what a great actress she was, then added that she hated men to the point of not even speaking to men other than at work. I remember stories that made me smile and stories that disappointed me because they changed my image of some of my heroes.

One night after watching TV, Lloyd asked me if I wanted to take a ride. It was about 2:00 a.m. and we got into Mell's Aston Martin. Lloyd told me that they took her car into a Beverly Hills dealer that had the most highly-recommended Aston Martin mechanics in the area. They had to leave it overnight about once a month because it would start running rough and was hard to start. The next day it would run just great. After many visits, a mechanic took Lloyd aside and told him that he had spent too much money at the dealership. It seemed that all they did was take the car out late at night, on the freeway, and would "blow its nose." Mell only drove this high-powered car to the market, or to get her nails done. The whole system would get clogged with carbon. Lloyd and I headed for the freeway and were "blowing the nose" of this Aston Martin at just over 100 miles per hour when the lights and siren of a highway patrolman came out of nowhere. The police officer recognized Lloyd and asked what he was doing. Lloyd explained, and the officer was going to let him go with a warning. Lloyd actually argued with the officer and insisted that he get a ticket because he did break the law. He got the ticket and I was sworn to never tell Mell. She thought Lloyd was still taking her car to the dealership. It turned out that Lloyd had done this two or three times before, but hadn't gotten caught. He never did it again.

Don gives us insight into Mrs. Nolan's character:

> Mell was a beautiful woman and very, very proper
> most of the time. She was always in a dress, always
> with her hair in a unique double bun, without a single
> hair out of place. She always carried her hands folded
> and above her waist so that she would not develop
> veins in her hands. She had very strong opinions
> about almost everything and loved to explain why
> you were not correct if your opinion did not match
> hers. She was also deeply in love and devoted to her
> husband and family.

She still held a very cherished place in her heart for her late father.
Beside the mirror of her restroom was a framed snapshot of him. He
was, thus, the first person she would see each morning.

> After Melinda and I had been dating a few months,
> Mell realized that I was going to be more than just
> a friend to Melinda. She asked me to sit with her by
> the pool and very directly told me that I was not the
> type of person that she or Lloyd would pick for their
> daughter. She then named a couple of young men
> that she felt would be more suitable. I think she was
> trying to get me to just go away.

Nevertheless, Lloyd always made Don feel welcome and showed
him much respect. "When Melinda and I would be in the basement
watching TV or movies, he always coughed before coming down-
stairs to say goodnight—my clue that it was time to go home."

Mell was very proud of her first name (possibly named after her father?), but got very upset when people would spell it with one L. Some would argue with her that Mell with two Ls was for a man; therefore, she must be mistaken to be spelling it that way. On a whim, I started spelling it, on birthday cards or thank you notes to her, with 3 Ls. I explained one extra to make up for the Ls left off by her friends. She smiled but never said a word. I think it was the first thing I ever did that pleased her.

The Bel-Air fire of 1961 brought about a major change in my relationship with my future mother-in-law. I was up at their house at the time that police and fire officials came by and told everyone to prepare to evacuate on a 10-15-minute notice. We watched a lot of neighbors throw things in cars and leave. Mell decided we would not leave without a fight. It was a shock to all of us to see this lovely woman in a dress standing on the pitched roof of their huge home, wetting down any flying embers with the garden hose. The winds from the fire were so strong that books from homes that had exploded were flying through the air on fire. They didn't have a chance against Mell and her garden hose. Sometime during this confusion, she appeared with a pair of Lloyd's trousers on under her dress. I guess that she realized that being on a roof where people could see up her dress was not proper, even if you are fighting a fire. The rest of us were trying to save what we could of the house contents. I don't know who thought of it, but we started throwing silver, china and crystal in the pool. We would carry stacks of plates out of the house and flip them like Frisbees across the water. The crystal was placed piece by piece carefully in the water and allowed to float to the bottom. We had already dumped drawers full of silver in the pool. As a last-minute thought, all of Mell's and Melinda's jewelry was dumped in the pool. Mell wanted to do what we could to save her books. Lloyd and I got a big tarp from the garage and spread it out in the living room; and Lloyd, Mell, Melinda, and I started unloading the ceiling-high bookshelves onto this tarp. We were just finishing when Henry, their Japanese gardener, came up the driveway. When he saw what we were doing, he asked us two questions that had us all laughing and feeling foolish: How are you going to pull that tarp through the door? What are we going to use to pull the tarp? We had not thought of the size or weight of those hundreds of books. Henry then set up a site on the front lawn and we started moving books again. We spent the night sleeping on the living room floor with lights on. No one wanted to get too far away from escape or take the chance of missing the evacuation notice. The pool water was black with soot and ash, and Melinda and I dove for days retrieving all that we threw in the pool. We received a nice thank-you letter from the insurance company, who was more than glad to pay for cleaning rather than replacement. Only five long-stemmed crystal glasses broke. A day or so after the fire, the *Los Angeles Times* had a nice big picture of Melinda's old boyfriend "rescuing" a large TV from a burning home. This was the last time Mell ever mentioned him. It turned out he wasn't "rescuing," he was looting.

Don found that Mell had a sense of humor, too:

Mell was insistent that you always spoke and acted with proper manners. This was especially important when in a public place. This strong belief of Mell's made situations even funnier when things went wrong. Once, the four of us were having dinner at the Brown Derby in Hollywood. We were all at our best behavior, but Mell became quiet and you could see great irritation on her face. Lloyd asked what was wrong. Mell said, "Every time I look up, that old gray-haired biddy across from us is staring at me." Lloyd turned around and Melinda and I looked. It took us a few seconds to respond, but Lloyd suddenly laughed real loud and said, "Sweetheart, that's a mirror." I must admit I was surprised that she found that very funny, even if she was embarrassed.

Then there was the faux-pas that Mell did not see as funny:

Photographer--Bob Grosh

After the Bel-Air fire, a TV crew came to their house to film a talk show. The filming of a tour of the house and garden was finished, and Melinda and I were invited to join Mell and Lloyd on the couch to discuss our parts in saving things during the fire. They had already finished discussing the Emmy that Lloyd had won for his portrayal of Captain Queeg on *The Hallmark Hall of Fame* production of "The Caine Mutiny Court Martial." He had also played the same part on Broadway and in London for several years. Captain Queeg was a disturbed character who fumbled with ball bearings when under tension. Lloyd had

He always got a warm welcome home from Mell
when work took him away on location

the ball bearings welded together on a short chain so
he wouldn't accidentally drop them on stage. These
were kept on a hook, just below his Emmy in his bar.
During the interview, the host asked if any of us did
something silly like leave something valuable in order to save something meaningless, like a bowl of
fruit. Mell jumped at this question. "Oh, yes," she
said. "The first thing I did was run into Nolie's bar
and grab his balls." Lloyd, the true professional, covered greatly by switching all conversation back to the
play. Melinda and I slid to the floor and crawled out
of the room. The cameraman was trying to not laugh,
but his camera was shaking a lot. This incident was
never, ever discussed or mentioned.

1962 presented Lloyd with a role unlike any other he'd ever
had—Father of the Bride. How did he feel about this new part? He
told reporter Art Ryon that it was "a strange role—financially, you're
a hero; socially, you're a heavy and should stay in the wings." And, still
slim and unlined, though suavely gray-haired, a handsome father-of-
the-bride he was!

The wedding took place in the garden of the family home on October 27. Lloyd's little Melinda was now Mrs. Donald Lightfoot.

Also in 1962, Lloyd spent some more time in Europe, much of it
professional. He played Admiral Ryan in a British comedy called *We
Joined the Navy*. Kenneth More and another American actress, Joan
O'Brien, starred, with cameos by Mischa Auer, Dirk Bogarde and Sid

James. This marked the film debut of David Warner. It would not be seen in the US until 1965. Lloyd's next film in the UK brought him back to a recognizable role. One that he would enjoy.

CHAPTER 15

Hunting Girls with the Hammer

The character of Mike Hammer, created by Mickey Spillane in 1946, has become an icon of detective fiction. Several years ago, Mickey proclaimed on the radio program *Silver Screen Audio*, "Hammer has been the most translated writer in the world behind Lenin, Tolstoy, Gorki, and Jules Verne. And they're all dead." (Unfortunately, Mickey died on July 17, 2006, just after his appearance on the show.)

Mike Hammer was the prototype for the contemporary fictional detective. He was tough, smart, violent, and experienced. He did not have the weariness of Raymond Chandler's Philip Marlowe, or the conceit of Dashiell Hammett's Sam Spade.

You might argue that Mike Hammer was the world's oldest Baby Boomer.

After serving in WWII as a flight instructor in Greenwood Mississippi, Spillane returned to native New York.

Needing a mere thousand dollars to purchase a plot of land, Spillane decided to write a hardboiled detective story. He based his protagonist, Mike Hammer, on the comic strip character Mike Danger and named his book *I, The Jury*. While the hardcover edition didn't sell many copies, the paperback edition did good business. Good enough not only to earn Spillane his thousand, but also to convince him to continue writing Hammer novels. Mike's most recent adventure was published posthumously in 2006.

Hammer was first brought to the screen in 1953. Fittingly, his first appearance on printed page was his first on celluloid, *I, The Jury*." Biff Elliot, a young Broadway actor, was brought to Hollywood by producer Victor Saville to play Hammer. Elliot was surrounded by a great supporting cast which included Peggie Castle, Preston Foster, Margaret Sheridan and Alan Reed. The film was photographed by one of the great cinematographers, John Alton; and the music was composed by the legendary Franz Waxman. It was shot in 3-D, but only released in a flat print. (A 3-D print does exist and it is shown at 3-D film festivals.) Armand Assante played Hammer in the 1985 remake.

Three years later, Saville produced *Kiss Me Deadly*, this time with veteran character actor Ralph Meeker as Hammer. This was a tough, violent and uncompromising film, years ahead of its time. The film also had a strong supporting cast, including Albert Dekker, Fortunio Bonanova, Nick Dennis, Juano Hernandez, and Paul Stewart. Topnotch film heavies Jack Lambert and Jack Elam spent a lot of time menacing Hammer, who was surrounded by a bevy of beauties that included Cloris Leachman (in her first film role), Gaby Rodgers, Marion Carr, and Maxine Cooper. Robert Aldrich directed it, using many unique touches. The final product was so brutally dark that, upon seeing it, French critics dubbed it *film noir*, setting a new genre of film.

Robert Bray, in *My Gun Is Quick*, also played Hammer on the silver screen.

More popularity came Hammer's way in the form of television. Revue Productions syndicated a television series that starred Darren McGavin in seventy-eight episodes that ran from January, 1958, through September, 1959. It was a crudely-produced show, but it was popular. Spillane had no involvement in the series.

Spillane was never quite satisfied with the way Hammer was portrayed on the screen. Despite the popularity of *Kiss Me Deadly*, Spillane didn't like it. Continuing with his radio interview, Spillane complained, "That guy Bezzerides (scenarist A.I. Bezzerides) ended the film with the Atom Bomb going off. I would never write anything like that." Spillane thought just as little of Hollywood in general. "The only guy who knew anything about movies was Duke Wayne. He hired me to go into a picture and play myself. He never interfered." The film was *Ring of Fear,* where Mickey played himself trying to find a killer sabotaging Clyde Beatty's circus. The picture was a failure, but nine years later Spillane used his experience as a thespian as a way to at least satisfy his desire to portray Hammer as he saw him. The picture was *The Girl Hunters,* based on Spillane's most recent novel at the time. Spillane himself played Hammer, who has become a drunk after the disappearance of Velda, his girl Friday. He is finally sobered up by his friend Captain Pat Chambers (Scott Peters), who wants him to question a dying sailor who was shot with the same gun that killed a U. S. senator. He is joined in a search for the killer by Federal Agent Art Rickerby (Lloyd) and is helped by real-life columnist Hy Gardner (himself). Hammer meets up with the senator's beautiful widow (Shirley Eaton, who would shortly score big time as the gold-painted victim in the James Bond caper *Goldfinger*). There are more murders, much violence and a typical Spillane ending.

The film was produced by Robert Fellows, who was John Wayne's partner when *Ring of Fear* was made. Roy Rowland, who had known Lloyd since their days at MGM when Lloyd was doing films and Rowland was directing many of the award-winning MGM shorts and would eventually become a feature director, was the director of this film shot entirely in England, even though it is set in the United States. He and Lloyd were good friends. Rowland's son Steve recalls his father's relationship with Lloyd: "My father really liked him. They were great friends. Dad thought of him as a total professional." One of the reasons might have been the passion they both had for the game of golf. Both were low-handicap golfers.

While Spillane had the best feel for how Hammer was to be played, he was not a trained actor and it showed. The film was rescued by Nolan's great performance as Rickerby and Eaton's Laura Knapp. The story and screenplay was an asset as well.

Spillane was not through with acting. In 1995, he appeared in two Max Alan Collins films, playing an attorney.

Spillane continued to bask in the growing popularity of Mike Hammer. A chance meeting on an airplane with super-agent Jay Bernstein resulted in the most recent incarnation of Mike Hammer. The first effort was a 1981 made-for-TV feature called *Margin for Murder*. Kevin Dobson was Hammer. It was well-received and Bernstein, now the rights holder of the Hammer character and the film's executive producer, made plans for a sequel. He made some casting changes in the follow-up, called *More Than Murder*. He hired Stacy Keach to play Hammer, Lindsay Bloom to play Velda, Don Stroud to play Pat Chambers, and Kent Williams to play Assistant District Attorney Lawrence Barrington. The success of this film and the follow-up, *Mur-*

der Me, Murder You, led to a full sixty-minute television series that ran on CBS for forty-six episodes, from 1984 to 1987. Despite the fact that, during the run of it, Keach was incarcerated for nine months in an England prison for cocaine possession and was off the air, Hammer was accepted back after serving his sentence, and the show ran an additional season.

Bornstein, Keach, and the rest of the stock company were not involved in the 1994 TV movie *Come Die With Me.* Rob Estes was Hammer and Pamela Anderson was Velda. Spillane's involvement was as the creator of the Mike Hammer character.

Jay Bernstein Productions was not through with Mike Hammer. Keach starred in twenty-six episodes that aired from September, 1997, through June, 1998.

Lloyd stayed in Europe to unite with John Wayne in *Circus World.* In the film he was joined by film veterans Rita Hayworth and Richard Conte. Claudia Cardinale and John Smith played the young lovers. Lloyd's old director buddy Henry Hathaway was in charge. The film was shot in Cinerama and the highlight was a fire.

Back in the States, Lloyd was given the role of Mayor Crane in the film version of the Broadway smash hit *Never Too Late,* which ran for three years and over 1,000 performances. Paul Ford, whose star was reborn after playing Colonel Hall in the TV hit *The Phil Silvers Show,* and Maureen O'Sullivan, best known as Tarzan's original Jane, recreated their stage roles playing a fifty-something couple who find out that they will be parents again. They have a son-in-law and daughter (Jim Hutton and Connie Stevens) living with them, trying to duplicate the process. Lloyd plays the mayor of the town in which the couples live.

Harry (Paul Ford) doesn't seem to relish the joke by Mayor Crane (Lloyd) but Harry's wife (Maureen O'Sullivan) does, in *Never Too Late*

On January 18, 1965, Lloyd delivered the eulogy for his friend, Jeanette MacDonald. They had known each other since working on her final film, *The Sun Comes Up*, together in 1949, and they had appeared together when Roy Rogers was given a safety award over a decade earlier.

An American Dream (1966) represented a happy reunion for Lloyd. One of his co-stars was Barry Sullivan, who had replaced Henry Fonda as Barney Greenwald in *The Caine Mutiny Court Martial*. The film was directed by Robert Gist, who had played Tom Keefer in the same production. Lloyd played Barney Kelly, the father of a woman (Eleanor Parker) who is murdered by her estranged husband (Stuart Whitman), who is a television commentator. In a bit of offbeat casting, one of the villains was played by Les Crane, a *real* talk show host.

Jeanette presents Roy with his award. With them are Gabby Hayes, Dr. Wayne Hughes, Margaret O'Brien, Lloyd, and Maureen O'Sullivan. (From the collection of Eleanor Knowles Dugan)

In England, Lloyd appeared in another thriller, *The Double Man* (1967), which starred Yul Brynner. He then appeared as part of an all-star cast in *Sergeant Ryker* (1968). Lee Marvin starred in the title role, and he was joined by Lloyd, Vera Miles, Bradford Dillman, Peter Graves, Murray Hamilton, and Norman Fell. Another ensemble piece was *Ice Station Zebra*, a big-budget John Sturges production that starred Rock Hudson, Ernest Borgnine, Patrick McGoohan, and former NFL star Jim Brown. In this Cold War drama, Lloyd plays Admiral Garvey, who sends Hudson's nuclear-power submarine to a British North Pole weather station to recover a capsule from a downed Russian satellite, which was taking photographs of US missile sites.

Ross Hunter called upon Lloyd's services again for his all-star blockbuster, *Airport*, based on Arthur Hailey's smash novel. Lloyd

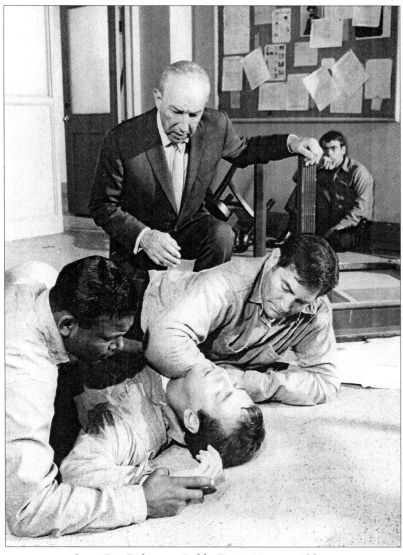

Sugar Ray Robinson, Bobby Darin, Norman Alden,
Lloyd, and Dean Stockwell in *The Danny Thomas Hour* "The Cage."

was honored to be part of a cast that included Burt Lancaster, Dean Martin, Dana Wynter, Jacqueline Bisset, Jean Seberg, Helen Hayes, Barbara Hale, Maureen Stapleton, and Van Heflin in his last film.

Lloyd played a customs inspector who thinks that Heflin is acting strangely in one of the many subplots of the film that centers on an airport manager (Lancaster).

Despite the pure soap opera plot, *Airport* was an enormous success. It received ten Academy Award nominations, winning a statuette for Helen Hayes.

Lloyd continued to do television work. He was enjoying the "guest star" status and assumed that, other than an occasional film, this would be how he would finish his career.

He couldn't have been more inaccurate.

CHAPTER 16

Julia

Lloyd considered himself semi-retired, so was very reluctant to take on the demanding schedule that being a regular on the weekly television show would require. Having been burned in the past with television contracts he regretted, he would not consider an offer until after he had read the script.

The show's producer, Hal Kanter, considered Lloyd the "Rolls-Royce of actors." He wanted him on that show badly enough that he not only gave him the script for his consideration, but was also willing to make many unusual concessions for him. Through Lloyd's agent, Bill Robinson, they negotiated the terms—Lloyd would only have to work forty-four days per year, and he would get special billing as "Frequently Starring Lloyd Nolan" in each and every episode, even though he would not appear in all episodes.

"This is the finest contract I've ever had," Lloyd told *TV Radio Talk* reporter Joseph Curreri. "They arrange the schedule so that I can come on the set and start working immediately. This way there will be a maximum of work and a minimum of waiting. And they also agreed to write me out when I want out, and this is essential to me."

The money was good, too.

"It's almost a shame to take the money, though, since I seem to work only about one day a week," he said.

Best of all, this would be a ground-breaking television series in which a black actress, Diahann Carroll, would star as its title character, a beautiful and sophisticated nurse. Lloyd was all in favor of equal rights for both women and minorities, so he signed on the dotted line and became the star's grouchy boss, Dr. Chegley. "He is a doctor, hardnosed and quarrelsome, but with a heart as big as his gruff voice," explained Lloyd. "It's a beautiful role, the kind that comes along too seldom for any actor." The show made its point about race issues without being preachy.

In his book, *So Far, So Funny*, Kanter wrote, "Nolan loved the script and breathed life into his role of Dr. Chegley. He and Diahann got along splendidly; even though Lloyd was so Republican we had to shoot around him when he went to Washington as the president's guest for Nixon's inauguration. Di was not." So Republican was Lloyd, in fact, that he received signed books from both Richard Nixon and Ronald Reagan.

The show would make its debut in 1968.

From the very beginning, the issue of race relations was handled head-on, as evidenced by the phone conversation between nurse and doctor, prior to their first meeting.

Julia Baker:	"Did they tell you I'm colored?"
Dr. Chegley:	"What color are you?"
Julia Baker:	"Why, I'm Negro."
Dr. Chegley:	"Have you always been a Negro, or are you just trying to be fashionable?"

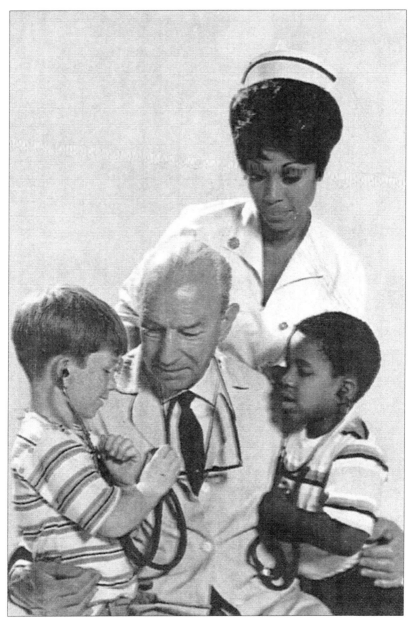

**Working with Diahann Carroll, Marc Copage, and
Michael Link in this series was a pleasure**

The no-nonsense Dr. Chegley

As the great Bill Cosby can attest, humor can do more to promote goodwill among all people than preaching can.

Series creator/producer/writer Hal Kanter had much respect for Lloyd. "Every once in a while he'll suggest we can eliminate some words," he told *TV Guide* reporter Robert de Roos. "'I can say the same thing with a gesture or a look,' he says. Not many actors will do that. They're always after more words. Then, if they're lousy, they can blame the writer.'"

Lloyd had a quiet, respectful way with people; and he was patient with the children on the show, as well. As a consequence of this, his co-workers would, more often than not, follow through on his suggestions.

In *Julia's* second season, Lloyd agreed to work more days, so Kanter added a new character to the show – Dr. Chegley's elderly uncle. For that, Lloyd would play a dual role. Kanter said, "For the first time since he's been on the show, he asked to see the dailies and he sat there chuckling all the way through. He told me, 'This is the first time I can remember laughing at myself on the screen.'"

So successful was this show that Lloyd was nominated for an Emmy as Outstanding Continued Performance by an Actor in a Leading Role in a Comedy Series, and Diahann Carroll won the Golden Globe as Best TV Star—Female. It also was surely a big factor in the creation of a star for Lloyd's television work on the Hollywood Walk of Fame, located at 1750 Vine.

☆☆☆

Lloyd knew that smoking was bad for him and he wanted to quit, so he developed a system. He would buy a pack of cigarettes during the noon hour and at night he'd submerge the cigarettes that were

Mell and Lloyd were living the good life
(From the collection of Nolan Lightfoot)

remaining. Perhaps that would give him the smoking pleasure he en-joyed while lessening the damage it could do to his health.

Being rather busy these days, Lloyd and Mell changed the scope of their vacations. No longer were they making major trips to Europe once or twice a year. Now, it was shorter jaunts to the Far East, Mex-ico, and other points of interest. He always took his movie camera along and got some great footage of their adventures.

And, of course, they made frequent trips to Philadelphia to see Jay. Once, with rented car and picnic goodies, they had picked him up for a pleasant afternoon together. The staff had forgotten to mention to Mell and Lloyd that Jay had a new fetish. As the car zipped down the highway toward their destination, they didn't realize anything was amiss until they turned around to see how Jay was doing in the back-seat and discovered that he was now wearing nothing but an innocent

smile. He had tossed his clothes out the window along the way.

Never a dull moment!

Their large home was filled with antiques, as well as modern art and souvenirs from their many trips. Among the antiques was Lloyd's gun collection in a gun case reputed to have been owned by Jesse James. Outdoors, gorgeous azaleas, camellias and calla lilies were abundant, and there was nary a weed in their perfectly-manicured lawn, thanks to their talented gardener.

Lloyd and Mell might have been soul-mates, but they were able to sleep more soundly in separate bedrooms. That had been their practice throughout their marriage, and it worked for them.

Lloyd had become quite adept at real estate. For $100,000, he had bought 120 San Fernando Valley acres, then sold it for a cool million;

and he currently owned the apartment house in which Melinda and Don lived.

Mell was an excellent cook, much to Lloyd's delight. One of her favorite things was to give Sunday parties. Their only domestic employee was a twice-a-week cleaning lady, and that's the way Mell wanted it. She could handle everything else herself.

Lloyd's showbiz friends were important to him, as well. Among his favorites were Leon Ames, Pat O'Brien, Phyllis Diller, and Gene Raymond.

Now that Lloyd was a regular on a popular television show, he was more easily recognized when in public. He would regularly attend Los Angeles Rams games and had his own seat there. That's where fans would often find him. "It makes me feel good," he said to *TV Guide* reporter Robert de Roos, "when someone says, 'Thank you for all the pleasure you've given me over the years'—that's an extra dividend." His fame would often result in excellent service at restaurants around the world, as well.

Reporter de Roos also spoke to Lloyd's agent, Bill Robinson, who said of his client, "He's a gentle man and a gentleman..... I've represented him ten years and I don't even have a contract with him. That's unheard of!"

Don was helping his father-in-law move boxes and sort items to be given for their church's thrift store one day. It was a day he'd never forget.

> [Lloyd] found a leather case in one box and was surprised to find a pistol that he had purchased for Mell many years before. He thought that she needed protection for her and the kids while he was away on location or doing a play in Europe or New York. She

would not allow it in the house and he had not seen it for many years. He removed the pistol from its case and, while examining it, he pulled the trigger. It was loaded and the bullet was bouncing off of the walls, ceiling and floor while Lloyd and I immediately hugged the floor and both trying to make ourselves as small of a target as possible. I don't remember how many times I heard the bullet zing by me, but I do remember that neither Lloyd nor I could speak when it finally went quiet. Lloyd took the gun to the local police station and *gave* it to them. He didn't want it around his home, and that day was another agreed item that was never told to Mell.

One thing that greatly impressed Don was Lloyd's calm and controlled nature. He cites two examples:

Driving down the freeway, Lloyd cut a man off on an off-ramp by accident. It wasn't really Lloyd's fault as the man had been changing lanes frequently and wanted the space that Lloyd had just changed into. The man was stopped behind us at a light but managed to work his way into the next lane and pull up next to us. He rolled down his window and started calling Lloyd all kinds of names and making threats. This didn't sit well with me (a former marine), plus with Mell and Melinda in the car, I was ready to do whatever had to be done with this guy. Lloyd just looked straight ahead. The man continued his yelling.

Lloyd rolled down his window and looked at the man and softly said, "God bless you." The man looked surprised but said, "What?" Lloyd said, in a friendly, but louder, voice, "God bless you." The light changed and Lloyd drove across the intersection. I looked back and the man was still sitting at the now-green light.

Once while sitting out by the pool, we were all surprised by golf balls flying by and hitting the house. Lloyd said he would get it stopped. He drove around the block and found a young man driving golf balls down his driveway. He complimented the young man on his great drive and explained the problem to his parents, then he invited him to play golf with him at the Bel-Air Country Club. Problem solved.

Speaking of golf, Lloyd showed up at the doctor's office where Melinda worked and complained of just not having any energy. The doctor examined him and gave him a shot of Vitamin B. For several weeks after that, Lloyd would drop in for a Vitamin B shot. Finally, the doctor told him that this loss of energy could be serious and they should look into more testing to see what was causing it. Lloyd confessed that his lack of energy wasn't really ongoing, but, after that first day of getting a Vitamin B shot, he played the best golf he had ever played and continued to play that well if he got a "B" shot each morning before golf.

One day in January of 1969 the telephone rang. Lloyd answered it. He received devastating news: their son Jay had choked on a bit of meat and died. The Heimlich Maneuver would come into being in 1974, but was not known when Jay needed it. Lloyd was heartbroken. Hanging up the phone, he dreaded giving the news to Mell. How would she handle it? She had to be told, though, so Lloyd phrased it as gently as he could.

Her response surprised him.

"Oh, thank God!" she said, with much relief. Mell had been praying for a long time that God would either cure Jay or take him, so he wouldn't have to suffer any longer. Now she knew that he was safe and sound in his Maker's arms, his frustration ended, and nothing would ever hurt him again.

CHAPTER 17
A Cause is Waiting

Lloyd had to do something to keep grief from eating him up, so he channeled his energies into service. He was now determined to do everything he could to improve the lives of people with autism and their families. He followed in William Talman's and Dana Andrews' courageous footsteps and appeared in public service announcements to educate the public. Talman's was about his heavy smoking, which led to lung cancer, from which he was obviously dying; Andrews' was about his alcoholism, urging viewers to not drink and drive; Lloyd's was about Jay's autism. The more public awareness there was, the more funding autism's researchers would get.

In the midst of grief came a golden beam of sunshine. On February 24, 1970, Melinda and Don became parents of a son. They named him Nolan William Lightfoot, and Lloyd and Mell would greatly cherish their first grandchild.

Melinda and Don adored their son, too, but were having marital difficulties. They began divorce proceedings. Lloyd was sad at this turn of events and let Don know how much he enjoyed having him for a son-in-law.

Melinda, nicknamed "Merdock," was so proud of her
little boy (From the collection of Nolan Lightfoot)

Don Lightfoot and their son Nolan (From the collection of Nolan Lightfoot)

Grandpa was mighty fond of the little guy, too

Melinda then dated Tim Cairns. A bit younger than she, Tim liked to tease her about that. She fell in love with this gentleman and they married on January 22, 1972. Tim would raise little Nolan as his own. This marriage would endure for the rest of Melinda's life.

Not being a "movie person," Tim paid little attention to Lloyd's career. While he and Lloyd did have a pleasant relationship, it was Mell he remembers with great fondness. She was quite open to him, more so than Lloyd was. "She was an absolute delight," he says fondly.

It was in the early 1970s that Connie and Dr. Harvey Lapin came into Lloyd's life. They, too, have an autistic son. The tireless work of the Lapins and Nolans, together with that of other movers and shakers, greatly improved conditions for afflicted families. "We had a fundraiser for our group," says Harvey, "and we brought Lloyd with us. He was always willing to help."

A very powerful bond formed between Lloyd and Harvey, from day one.

"He'd come to all our fundraisers. He never, ever said 'no,'" he continues. "Lloyd was the first celebrity that came out for our kids." Lloyd would line up others—Charlton Heston, Bob Hope, Leon Ames, and Jack Klugman—to make appearances, as well.

Lloyd would call the Lapins at least weekly. He loved their children, including their autistic son Sean, and was something of a father figure to Harvey, who was Jay's age. The Nolans had a strawberry patch in their backyard, and Lloyd would sometimes take the Lapins' children back there to pick the sweet, juicy berries. "He was so kind," says Harvey. "He made us feel so special." The men would frequently have lunch together at the deli. When Harvey's parents would come visit, Lloyd would go to lunch with them. He got along quite well with the elder Lapin, even though the gentleman spoke no English.

And there was another endearing thing about Lloyd. "He'd cry in a blink," Harvey laughs, "the old Irishman." After a few drinks, Harvey and Lloyd would begin telling stories with an Irish brogue, and sometimes Lloyd's tears would begin. "You old crybaby," Mell would tease. Connie and Harvey would be invited to all of the Nolans' Christmas and Easter parties. The two couples would have so much fun together.

Lloyd narrated the 1973 documentary *Normalization: A Right to Respect* for the Atlanta Association for Retarded Children and Wooster Productions. This film enlightened viewers regarding the benefits of including disabled children in all areas of life—home, school, church, work, health care, entertainment, and elections. It was not pity or a free ride they wanted. All they wanted was a chance, and Lloyd was very willing to help make that happen.

He was to make a trip to the headquarters of the National Society for Autistic Children, known as NSAC (now renamed the Autism Society of America, ASA), staying overnight in New York City. NSAC board member Dennis Hansen, of Long Island, was there to meet him. The two men had an enjoyable evening, going first to dinner, then for a walk. Dennis remembers Lloyd as "very pleasant, down-to-earth, and very easy to talk to. He was recognized on the street, and it seemed to please him when people called his name. He would respond with a smile. No one was bold enough to actually approach him and that was appreciated, too."

Dennis' wife Carol adds, "Lloyd was concerned about the effect autism was having on families, particularly the mothers. This impressed Dennis . . . and me, too!"

The House of Representatives, Committee on Education and Labor, held their ninety-third Congress in 1973. Hearings on H.R. 4199, the amendment to extend the Education of the Handicapped Act for three years, were held before their Selection Subcommittee on Education March 9 and 21; and Lloyd was in Washington, D.C. to give his testimony, as was actor Tony Curtis, who had a brother and children with disabilities. Nolan and Curtis were accompanied by Mary Akerley, a member of the NSAC Board of Directors. Never before had Lloyd's aura of authority and respectability been so crucial to the wellbeing of so many people. Here is his testimony. (Errors of spelling and punctuation are copied verbatim from the transcript released by the U.S. Government Printing Office, Washington.)

Thank you, Mr. Chairman.

I would like to say I am very honored to be permitted to testify before your subcommittee.

I suppose I may be known to some of you as a stage and screen actor for the last half of this century. I am also the father of an autistic son who died 4 years ago at the age of 26, and I am the 1974 Honorary Chairman of the National Society of Autistic Children and a spokesman for the organization today.

Since autism is still so little known or understood even among the professionals, I ask the committee's indulgence to permit me to speak a bit about the problem itself before discussing the proposed legislation, and how it can help our children. We do not want to take up too much of your time and have, therefore, attached some supplementary material to our testimony.

Autism is very difficult to diagnose because it plays so many roles. Sometimes it appears to be mental retardation, sometimes emotional disturbance or psychosis, sometimes aphasia or some other learning disability. Strangely, these children almost without exception are beautiful children. My son was very handsome but there are certain telltale signs that set autism apart from other early childhood disorders. Autistic children seem like little robots; they are very compulsive, wanting everything in their daily routine repeated without any variation--those who do take notice of toys usually play with them inappropriately and in the same order day after day. They appear to want little or nothing to do with the world and its inhabitants, even their own families and their own mothers. They look through people, not at them. They cannot use or understand language; those who do speak do so like tape recorders: in a flat voice they endlessly repeat phrases or entire conversations they have heard earlier, usually on the radio or television. They cannot play imaginatively or imitatively--such play implies an awareness of and relation to the outside world.

They occupy themselves by spinning objects such as jar lids or by flapping their hands in front of their faces. I remember my son in the pool, hour after hour, would wet his hand and watch the water drip. He was watching the glare of the sun in the drops.

Dr. Lorna Wing, a British researcher, has observed that much of this symptomatology is also found in children born deaf-blind. There is a clue here: the autistic child, even though his vision and hearing are unimpaired--even acute--somehow cannot use the information they provide. In the midst of the richness of the sensory world, he remains in heartbreaking isolation.

I have painted a very dark picture; for many years it was completely black. The bit of light now making at least the general outlines discernible has come from special education and research. The burden of providing the former has rested chiefly on the parents of autistic children; most of the schools for autistic children in this country were started by desperate parents who had found every public educational door closed and locked to their children. Nor was any incentive to unlock those doors provided at the Federal level until very recently.

Two schools for autistic children, one on each coast, are currently participating in a joint project under the provisions of Public Law 91 230, whose renewal is being considered today. The goal of this project is to develop a national network of interested and cooperating agencies, serving the psychoeducational needs of severely emotionally disturbed children with particular attention to children who are autistic or psychotic. The hope would be for expansion of the network over several subsequent years with the joint team continuing to head up and coordinate the training, interrelated studies, and cooperative research.

That hope will die if the Education of the Handicapped Act dies. Once the first step into the light has been made, we cannot return to the dark. For the first time, autistic children are getting services under a piece of Federal legislation; true, it is only a small group of children, the population of two schools, and the services are really indirect as the thrust of the program is the development of teacher-training methods. But therein lies the greater hope, more and better trained teachers mean more and better programs and, consequently, more children served.

Since 1957 there have been several independent studies on the affectiveness of various types of treatment in alleviating the symptoms of autism; all have come to the same conclusion: autistic children who are in special education programs show marked improvement and a greater rate of progress than those who are not in school.

Mr. Chairman and members of the committee, H.R. 4199, which would extend the Education of the Handicapped Act for 3 years, deserves your favorable attention. I am sure you will not take away from our children what they have only recently been given.

One reason that autistic children have been excluded from so many special education programs is the lack of knowledge about proper techniques. We need more programs such as the BEH project just described, but we also need more schools.

On Monday, Congressman Harrington introduced the Autistic Children Research Act. While not on today's agenda, the matter of the bill is germane to today's topic; and since I have come such a long way to speak about the needs of autistic children, and since this is the first bill calling for services specifically for autistic children to be considered by the Congress, I ask the subcommittee's permission to testify on behalf of it as well.

Although entitled a "research act," the second section of the bill provides for Federal assistance to public or private educational centers, both day and residential, in the form of grants, loans or loan guarantees. The need for more schools can be demonstrated most effectively, I feel, by the experiences of two families whose situation is by no means unusual. Before telling you their stories, let me explain that an autistic child imposes a terrible strain, emotional and financial, on a family. The parents love the child but cannot reach him; they are often blamed by professionals for causing the condition which has broken their own hearts, and which they are trying so hard to remedy; there are either no appropriate services available or they are prohibitively expensive--tuitions range from $2,500 to $28,000 per years.

Incidentally, the breakup of marriages is 52 percent for parents of autistic children.

There is, or perhaps I should saw "was," a family in Maryland with an autistic son. I corrected my tense because now only the husband lives there; he remained behind because of his job when his wife and son, as well as their normal daughter, moved to Connecticut so that the boy could go to school. The poor man is now deprived of the comforts of family life and the joy of his normal child; he is exhausted from the physical strain of visiting his family on weekends and from the financial strain of maintaining two households.

The other family lives in Texas. Their autistic son goes to school in Missouri. The school involves parents very actively in the psychoeducational process, so the mother spends the week in St. Louis in order to participate, then goes home to Dallas on weekends.

I know what these families are going through. I live in California but our son had to go to school in Pennsylvania. The accident which took his life happened there--far away from his home and family.

There should be good day and residential programs for

autistic children in every State. Residential placement is sometimes the best way to provide the intensive services a child may need; however, it may, unfortunately, be chosen when not appropriate because there is no local day school. Hence, the need for both types of program, which could in many cases be provided in the same facility.

Ladies and gentlemen of the subcommittee, it was 30 years ago this year that Dr. Leo Kanner described "infantile autism" as a separate syndrome. That was just about the time that my son was born. Thirty years is a very long time to wait for help. And Mr. Harrington's bill does not ask for a great deal, especially when compared to other Federal education programs.

Thirty years ago the prognosis for autism was expressed in thirds: one-third of the victims made enough progress to live at least semi-independently if not "normally," one-third did progress out of their severely autistic state; and one-third remained mute and withdrawn. Now, with improved education and research techniques, the outlook is brighter, but to what avail if there are no centers for delivery of services?

What will happen to the family who cannot move to or commute to another State? An autistic child with no program is a restless, frustrated child; as he grows older his hyperactivity--his only way of handling his frustration--may become a destructive force, turned against himself or his environment. The strain of family life is indescribable; the effect on the other children, who are forced to watch their parents give all their attention to their seemingly spoiled, constantly misbehaving sibling, can be devastating.

We have before us a simple choice: educate autistic children, which is really just giving them their rights, or we can ignore them until they have to be institutionalized. The cost of the first choice could run as high as $50,000 per child; the cost of the second is $400,000 per child, plus the incalculable cost of broken families. But even if this were not so, passage of H.R. 4199 would be justified. Autism has been the stepchild of the handicaps. America has not taken adequate care of any of her handicapped children; we know that and are concerned about it, but she has shamefully neglected her autistic offspring--perhaps because there are so few--only 4 in 10,000--perhaps because so little is known about how to help them, perhaps because so many have disappeared into institutions for the retarded or insane.

Whatever the reason or reasons, this subcommittee has before it the opportunity to correct the long years of neglect. Fragmented though the research is, it has shown that autistic children are not retarded or mentally ill; they are constitutionally impaired. This research must be continued and expanded if we are ever to stop wasting a potentially valuable human resource. And this much we do know: autistic children can and must be educated. Passage of H.R. 4199 would insure that the first nationally supported tentative starts in that direction will not be aborted. Passage of the Autistic Children's Research Act would, in addition to making a powerful national commitment to research, make possible desperately needed day and residential educational facilities--the professionals trained under the BEH programs could carry out the network concept of those programs via the centers provided by this bill.

We have emphasized our children's needs today because this is the very first time Federal programs for them have been considered. We are very enthused about this new potential and hope we have communicated some of that enthusiasm to the subcommittee.

Thank you.

Lloyd's friend Harvey gave his testimony, as well. After these very intense meetings, it was time to relax. The two men attended the play *I Do, I Do,* starring Carol Burnett and Rock Hudson. Lloyd was very pleasantly surprised to see what a genuinely good actor Hudson was on stage. "He was really talented," he later told *L.A. Herald-Examiner's T.V. Weekly* reporter Frank Torrez. "For some reason, you just didn't expect him to be that good, but he was."

"Lloyd and Carol Burnett had the same business manager, so he knew her real well," says Harvey. They went backstage after the play to say "hello" to the star. As Burnett, Hudson, Nolan and Lapin left the building, autograph seekers asked them to sign their books. Getting into the spirit of things, Harvey signed the books, too. Lloyd stopped and said, "What're you doing?" Lapin grinned, "If you can do it, I can do it."

They had so much fun together. Back home, the two men would often go to Zukie's Deli in Santa Monica, where Lloyd would inevitably order a pastrami sandwich with a Heineken.

The next year, Lloyd was approached by officials of NSAC. They asked if he would serve as Honorary Chairman of their organization for the year 1974. He agreed, and continued to pour his heart and soul into the cause.

The positive results of Lloyd's and others' earlier testimony at the congressional hearing, along with his hard work in other ways, would be seen in the years ahead.

"I am convinced that 94-142 became national law because of the precedent set in California because of Lloyd Nolan," says Harvey. Public Law 94-142, called the Education of All Handicapped Children Act and passed in 1975, was a godsend to children with disabilities. This law guaranteed such a child free and appropriate education in the public school system. The era of shutting handicapped children away in attics or institutions was over; and these young, now-educated people would often grow up to be tax-paying citizens. This,

The engraved metal plate on the front of this photo's frame says, "Lloyd Nolan with Gov. Ronald Reagan signing first public education law in the United States for autistic children 1974" (From the collection of Nolan Lightfoot)

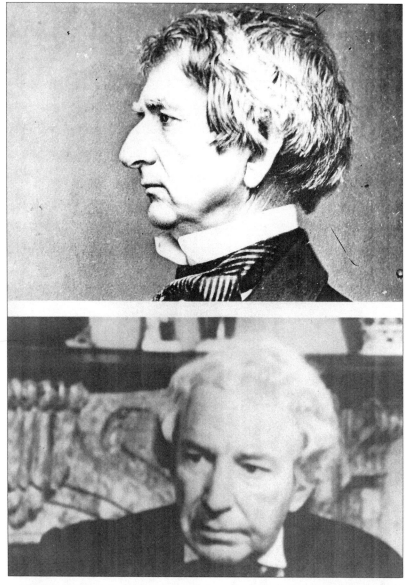

Amidst his tireless work for the disabled, Lloyd still took on acting jobs now and then. Such was the role of William H. Seward, who ran against Abraham Lincoln for the Republican nomination for president, but ended up serving in Lincoln's cabinet instead. The series was *Sandburg's Lincoln*; the episode was "The Unwilling Warrior." (Photographer of Seward portrait - Mathew Brady)

and the Developmental Disabilities Act, which took autism out of the mental-illness classification, did more for the cause than anything else. "It happened," Harvey says, "because Lloyd asked [then California Governor] Ronald Reagan to sign it and he did. That was the first in the nation."

So important were disabled people to Lloyd that he would even picket to keep politicians from cutting their programs.

Also in 1975 and with the Nolans' and Lapins' active participation, as well as that of Joanne Woodward and Paul Newman, the Autism Society of Los Angeles established the Jay Nolan Center. When asked earlier if it would be okay to name it after his son, Lloyd was touched. "I'd be honored," he said. The Center has grown and flourished over the years and is now called Jay Nolan Community Services, Inc. Its philosophy is that:

- All people have capacities and gifts.

- All people need a sense of belonging to a community.

- All people contribute to a community.

- All people can live in their own home with the right support.

- All people should be treated with dignity and respect and have a right to privacy.

- All people have the right to be heard and their ideas acknowledged.

This fine California organization is headquartered in Mission Hills, with branches in Los Angeles, San Jose, and Lancaster. It supports and helps people with autism and other developmental disabilities to live as full and productive a life as possible. It provides a world for them that is almost ideal.

Much of Lloyd's acting income would be donated to the Saugus branch of this organization.

From this parent organization came the Jay Nolan Camp, which brings together thirty-five children with disabilities and sixty-five without to have fun together in two six-day sessions each year. For these one hundred children, there are forty trained staff members to lead the hikes, crafts, archery sessions and other activities one would typically find at any camp. This not only gives children with disabilities to chance to interact in a positive way with regular, everyday people, but it also helps all of them to develop tolerance and patience as they realize how much they have in common. Quite often, the children who earlier came as campers will come back as counselors in later years. This is as close to a "perfect world" as children with disabilities are likely to ever see.

Dr. Ruth Sullivan, who is very active in the field of autism, first met Lloyd in Washington, DC, then again in Los Angeles. "I was impressed at his gentle spirit. It just came out. He was truly interested in talking to people, he met your eyes, he wanted to hear what you had to say," she says. "He was interested in a depth of conversation that was very charming."

The Nolans invited Dr. Sullivan to their home, and she accepted. "A kind and gracious person is how I thought of him. They treated us very well at their house, very gracious both of them." They went into the garden and Dr. Sullivan expressed an admiration for one of their exotic plants. "I loved it at the time, and he pulled some out of the ground and gave it to me. I just treasured that." She added, "That was very generous of him to do that!"

Autism wasn't understood by the public in the early 1970s. "We [NSAC] needed support of people who could confirm us as being legitimate, serious, worthwhile, worthy of attention. [Lloyd] came about at a very good time for us because autism was considered to be rare at that time. It was considered one in twenty-five hundred, and now is one hundred fifty."

The seemingly higher incidence of autism now might be because its definition has been greatly expanded to encompass a wider scope of disability.

"We were looking for people who had name recognition . . . and [Lloyd] was very happy to do that. He went out of his way to do that."

Dr. Sullivan recalls a meeting that she and San Diego University executive Anne Donnelan attended. Mell and Lloyd were there, as well, and the ladies noticed something endearing about Lloyd. "Under the table, he kind of put his hand over [Mell's] hand while he was sitting there. And we looked at each other and said, 'How sweet!' Who wouldn't kill for a man who does that? And these are not young people; these are people who have grown children!"

She noticed, too, that he cried easily when telling a sad story. When asked about that, he shrugged, "I cry at card tricks."

Lloyd returned to the screen after his *Julia* duties had kept him away for four years. It was a cameo on another all-star disaster flick, *Earthquake*. Charlton Heston and Ava Gardner this time headed the all-star cast that once again spotlighted on the special effects.

☆☆☆

A scene in *Earthquake* with Charlton Heston and Ava Gardner

In October, 1974, the Nolans were preparing for a round-the-world trip, beginning in India; but Lloyd took time away from last-minute preparations to welcome a seventeen-year-old fan into his home. Stone Wallace, who is now the biographer of such luminaries as Johnny Depp and George Raft, was impressed that Lloyd was so unlike many big stars of the day. Their association had begun with a fan letter, which Lloyd graciously answered, requesting that Stone call him "Lloyd" instead of the stuffy "Mr. Nolan." They wrote to each other occasionally, and Lloyd invited Stone to come see him when he was in the area. How glad Lloyd was that this was the day and the hour—because, he said, that got him out of the thankless chore of packing. Lloyd showed Stone around, then took him to his study upstairs, where they settled down to talk. How Lloyd enjoyed reminiscing about his career.

They discussed, for a while, his war films, *Bataan* and *Wake Island.* "They were intended to boost morale among our troops," Lloyd said. "Don't forget, those were the early days of the war, and our first efforts in the Pacific were hardly encouraging. The war was hitting a little too close to home. I was at that age where I was too young to enlist in World War I, and too old to be drafted into the Second World War. I hope my playing in these pictures served some purpose." Lloyd did, in fact, participate in at least one World War II training film for the US Army/Air Corps, as well. It was entitled *Resisting Enemy Interrogation* and was released in 1944. Arthur Kennedy was also listed in its credits.

Then they focused on the 1940 films *The House Across the Bay,* starring George Raft, and *Johnny Apollo,* starring Tyrone Power and Dorothy Lamour. Lloyd laughed, "Ty and I had a lot of fun pulling pranks on Dorothy in *Apollo,* and she was such a good sport. What I remember most about working with George is that he seemed to have difficulty interpreting lines. He wasn't stage-trained and, frankly, was never that comfortable in front of the camera, but at the time I worked with him, he was probably the biggest star on the Paramount lot, next to Gary Cooper."

Stone asked, "After years of playing gangsters, soldiers, and hard-boiled detectives, it must have been a welcome change to play Officer McShane in *A Tree Grows in Brooklyn."*

"My favorite film," Lloyd smiled, "along with *Abandon Ship* (1957), where I again co-starred with Ty Power. Elia Kazan and I had worked together as actors in a picture called *Blues in the Night* (1941). I was playing another gangster, and I think he was part of this traveling band. I was flattered when he later asked me to play in *Brooklyn*."

When asked what the highlights of his career were, Lloyd responded, "Mainly just the people I had the good fortune to work with. Directors like Tay Garnett, actors like Alan Ladd and Ty Power, Bob Preston, and Dorothy Lamour."

☆☆☆

Young Nolan was spending quite a bit of time with his "Omah" and "Bopah." Lloyd enjoyed his company and taught the boy how to swim. They even had a tree fort for him in Lloyd's front yard. The animals—Lloyd's dogs and parrot, and Mell's horses—were a big part of this home, as well. What a welcoming place for a child!

Fans, too, were recipients of Lloyd's caring concern. Here's a handwritten letter, dated August 6, 1976, that he wrote to one of them:

> Dear Dr. Braude: - Yes, I know how you feel. – I'll be 74 in a few days. We've lived through a lot of things, simultaneously, haven't we? World War I, the Depression, World War II, Nickelodeons, Movies, Talkies, Radio, T.V., the Era of flight – much more. It looks like many more exciting things are due in the near future, Mars, etc. Hope we're around to see them. If not, I hope we have good front seats up above.
>
> Again, thanks for the letter. It's always an added dividend to know one gave pleasure to people and that they still remember.

Think of all the good you've been able to do in your life – I'll bet plenty of people remember <u>that</u>!

Very sincere regards to you
from Lloyd Nolan

Another fan, Daphne Di Castri, in Canada, had written to him, too. Lloyd's warm response is shown above.

☆ ☆ ☆

One of the ways Lloyd was able to help those with autistic children was by narrating a twenty-five-minute documentary entitled *Minority of One*. In this film, he explained what autism is, how the children so afflicted struggle to understand the world, and the difficulties involved with parenting these children. If only the general public were more knowledgeable about the syndrome, they might react to autistic people with more kindness and understanding. Among those shown in this film was Lloyd's friend Connie Lapin. He also opened his family photo album to reveal beautiful photos of Jay.

When not doing charity work, Lloyd continued to work on television. Considering the large amount of "down time" in filmmaking and his aversion to boredom, it's logical that he would prefer the quicker pace of television shows. Quality roles were difficult to find, though. Scripts were often hurriedly written to keep up with this quick pace. Lloyd had so enjoyed working on *Julia* and would accept a regular role in another series like that in a heartbeat, but shows of that caliber were very rare.

Released in 1977 was a film titled *Fire*, which boasted many well-known stars in its cast: Lloyd, Ernest Borgnine, Vera Miles, Patty Duke, Alex Cord, Erik Estrada, Donna Mills, and Ty Harden, among others. "One great thing about being an actor," said Alex Cord, "is that you get to work with other actors that you're a fan of." Yes, those in the acting profession are often fans, too; and Alex had long admired the quality of Lloyd's performances. Cord regrets that the work on this film took most of their waking hours, so there was no time for socializing.

1977 saw another one of those all-star retro-cast films released to the big screen and an interesting farewell to a genre with which Lloyd had become synonymous. The film was *The Private Files of J. Edgar Hoover,* written, produced and directed by auteur Larry Cohen. For him, it was a dream come true. He related this story on the radio program *Silver Screen Audio:* "I had a great cast—Broderick Crawford (who played Hoover), Celeste Holm, Lloyd Nolan, Jose Ferrer, Dan Dailey, Howard Da Silva, Rip Torn, June Havoc. I really enjoyed working with all those actors, particularly the ones I'd seen as a child and had grown up with. I had said that someday I would work with these wonderful, wonderful players that I'd seen in my childhood and had been a part of my life. There I was directing them! I was shooting in Washington, DC." Still, despite this cast, Cohen was advised not to go through with the project. "Everybody told me 'Don't make this picture. You don't want to get on the wrong side of the F.B.I. People have been blacklisted; they didn't work for ten years. They have the power to raise their little finger and destroy your career. Nobody's ever made a picture critical of the F.B.I. before and you're crazy enough to want to shoot it in Washington, DC, and get shots in the F.B.I Offices, the training facility in Quantico, and even in J. Edgar Hoover's house. You're crazy.' And the truth was I was able to get to all of those locations and was able to shoot the first movie about the F.B.I that did not have F.B.I. pre-censorship."

In Cohen's mind, there was never any question that Lloyd would be a part of this project. "I told Lloyd Nolan that you can't make an F.B.I. movie without Lloyd Nolan. He said in that voice of his, 'That's very nice of you to say.' He had met Hoover once when he was making one of those F.B.I. pictures and he had said that he was very nice to him." Still, it wasn't easy for the now seventy-five-year-old actor. "He couldn't remember his lines. He had a lot of trouble with his lines. Eventually, I had to read his lines to him off stage. He kept apologizing. He'd say, 'Larry, I'm so sorry.' I finally said to him, 'Look, I'll just say the line and you repeat it.' We shot the other coverage with the other actor and put it together and it worked out just fine."

The incident jogged Larry Cohen's memory even further. "I remember that when I used to go down to NBC at 30 Rockefeller Plaza and they were doing live television, and Lloyd Nolan was doing *Martin Kane,* and I remembered that he could never remember his lines even then. The show was always off timing because Lloyd had to repeat his lines."

The film is an underrated masterpiece of sorts. For an old-time film buff, it is fun to see these icons of the forties reunited one more time, a little heavier, a little grayer, but still acting up a storm. It is Cohen's favorite of all the things he's done. Even though Lloyd did not play an F.B.I. agent in the film (he played Attorney General Harlan Stone), this was his final appearance in a film of this genre.

While many seasoned actors could be somewhat unpleasant to work with, that was certainly not the case with Lloyd. He was delighted to still be cast in acting roles. "He never complained or claimed special privilege," wrote William McPeak, who worked with him in television, in the mini-biography he wrote about Lloyd for the popular Internet Movie Database.

After a long, hot day at the studio, Lloyd couldn't wait to get home. When he did, one could find a trail of clothing between the car and the swimming pool as he relaxed and refreshed in the cool water. Once he'd had enough, he got out, put his clothes back on, and went into the house. Usually, daughter Melinda had a wonderful sense of humor. Today, though, it was nowhere in sight as she and her friends blushed from embarrassment from the pool.

Well, maybe their feelings about her dad weren't terribly positive right then, but Lloyd was greatly respected by his peers in entertainment and the world of autism. At the "Save Autistic Children Telethon" on December 10, 1977, Charlton Heston presented him with a plaque to honor both his fifty years in show business and his work to improve the lives of autistic children and their families. Lloyd would not only work hard on these fund and awareness raisers himself, but he'd frequently convince other celebrities to take part, too. Appearing at this particular telethon were Ernest Borgnine, Paul Newman, Joanne Woodward, and Beverly Sills. Monies raised would be channeled toward the establishment of a research facility there in Southern California, because state funding for programs benefiting autistic children had been scaled back.

Lloyd served as chairman of the annual Autistic Children's Telethon. Some, who worked on those shows too, have commented that he was fine while on the air but, when he was off-camera, he appeared very, very tired. Telethon work, because it continues for so many hours at a time, is exhausting to those who work on it continually. It is worth it, though. Dr. Lapin recalls one telethon that kept Lloyd up all night, but raised about $400,000 for the cause. "For others, it was a chore to help autism causes," he says. "For Lloyd, it was a labor of love."

Working on-camera like this in order to raise funds went against Lloyd's "Never tell anyone how to spend his money" philosophy. He always had a difficult time asking for anything. Nevertheless, the inspiration he got from the memory of his dear son was enough to keep him focused on the cause and its needs. He tried to get on television talk shows, too, but the "biggies" were not interested in his message. It was showbiz they wanted to talk about.

Along came Jack Klugman to the rescue.

It was on the sixty-minute *Quincy* series that Lloyd was able to combine his love for acting with his desire to increase public awareness about autism. The writer of the story and screenplay for this episode, entitled "A Test for the Living," was its star, Jack Klugman, who got his inspiration from the telethons on which he'd seen Lloyd. Aired on October 19, 1978, it is deftly described by Hal Erickson's *All Movie Guide* this way:

> No murder is committed nor autopsy performed in this episode, in which medical examiner Quincy (Jack Klugman) delves into psychology. The catalyst for the plot is Timmy Carson (David Hollander), a hyperactive seven-year-old with a severely limited attention span. Though Timmy has escaped from an institution for mentally retarded youngsters, Quincy is persuaded that the boy is actually suffering from a treatable form of autism. The problem now is to convince the authorities that the boy is not retarded— and to persuade Timmy's parents that the money needed to treat his autism will be worth spending. Featured in the guest cast is Lloyd Nolan, in real life the father of an autistic son, and a very young Tracey Gold as Timmy's sister.

Lloyd had blazed the trail. Autism was now an "in" cause, so others picked up the baton and ran with it.

Lloyd, Joe Campanella, Joanne Woodward, and Harvey Lapin at the "Save
Autistic Children Telethon" 1979 (Courtesy the Lapin Family)

"Mell was very strong in metaphysical beliefs," recalls Don Lightfoot. She felt that stressing the positive while ignoring the negative
promoted health. "A lot of Mell's inspiration came from the writings
of Mary Baker Eddy, the founder of Christian Science of the Mind
Church. When their housekeeper, Florence, developed a large stomach ulcer and was scheduled for surgery, Mell immediately put the
woman on a regimen of freshly-made cabbage juice, a glassful every
morning. That seemed to do the trick. On the day Florence was to
have surgery, they x-rayed to determine the size of her ulcer—and it
was gone without a trace!

Mell later revealed that she herself had had breast cancer, but had conquered it metaphysically. At first, Don and Melinda were skeptical. Mell showed them her diagnostic x-rays from a decade before, though, and they were convinced.

Sadly, she wouldn't be as fortunate next time, when the cancer recurred.

CHAPTER 18
Great Loss, New Beginnings

Grandson Nolan spent much time with Lloyd and Mell. He'd spend long weekends and long vacations at their house, flying from Colorado to California alone. In early 1980, his pregnant mother was bedridden, so he went to live for a time with them.

"When I was a kid," he recalls, "I knew when it was 9:00 in the morning the entire time I knew him because my grandmother would prop a newspaper up on the newspaper stand. There'd be a glass of juice, a quarter cantaloupe with yogurt, granola and fruit waiting for him. At 9:00 on the dot, you'd hear him shuffling down the stairs. He'd come and he'd read his paper. Afterwards, he'd get up, go to the refrigerator and he'd get a little spoon of horseradish. His eyes would water and he'd blow his nose, and he'd get going."

Lloyd wasn't known for being an easygoing driver. A bit aggressive, was he? Yes, indeed. He was confident that no one would want to hit a $250,000 Rolls-Royce, so other drivers would be extra alert with him around.

Nolan noticed something else interesting about his granddad, too. When he was at a celebrity event, he would see which door the big stars were using for their exit, and he would take another door.

Lloyd's Rolls (From the collection of Nolan Lightfoot)

Thus, he avoided the cameras. "He truly liked acting," Nolan says. "He didn't need all the other stuff that came with it."

Lloyd loved his grandson tremendously, but there were times that he had to be firm with him. Nolan reminisces, "I remember being about eleven in his little bar. There was this pistol on the wall and I grabbed it and fired two blank shots in the ceiling. Did I get it from that man! He let me have it, in that voice. When he'd get angry, I'd just stand there and take it."

January 6, 1981, was a bleak day for Lloyd and his family. That was the day that he lost his beloved Mell. She died at home of the breast cancer she had once conquered. Their beautiful garden had been the setting for Melinda's wedding, but now it would host a much sadder occasion—the family memorial service for Mell. Their marriage, Lloyd felt, had been practically perfect. Life just wouldn't be the same anymore without his sweetheart, and it was a year before he began working again.

A couple of years earlier, he had been interviewed by Ron De-Sourdis for a book he and co-author Marilyn Henry were writing about Alan Ladd, and Lloyd had been very generous in sharing his memories with him. During that interview, Lloyd had casually mentioned that he loved writing. Perhaps helping a bit with the resulting book, *The Films of Alan Ladd*, was just the distraction Lloyd needed at such a sad time. After all, he and Ladd had worked together in three films—*Gangs of Chicago, Wild Harvest,* and *Santiago*; and he had been very fond of the man. Author Marilyn Henry had been a fan of Lloyd's since the 1940s, so was delighted when he agreed to write the book's Introduction. Here, with the kind permission of the book's authors, is what Lloyd wrote about his pal:

> I first met Alan Ladd at Paramount studios in the cast of *Wild Harvest* in August 1947. The cast was a good group: Dorothy Lamour, Robert Preston, Allen Jenkins, Tony Caruso; and the director was that wonderful ex-newspaperman Tay Garnett.
>
> The picture was shot under not-so-usual circumstances—a studio strike was threatened by one of the branches of studio workers, and if a picket line were thrown up around the studio, our picture would have to close down. To eliminate this possibility, the chief members of the cast were asked to live at the studio. Spending five or six days glued together on a hot set, having three meals a day at the same long table in the commissary,

yakking over drinks until bedtime—you either became close friends or you collected some new enemies. Alan and I became friends—and stayed that way.

Alan's home was just about the halfway point between Hollywood and my home, and hardly a week went by that I didn't drop in for a quick one. I never had any fear of intruding, for Alan loved company, friends—though he was shy of strangers and avoided crowds. His dislike of crowds was well founded. The impression that Alan stood at least six-feet-plus was so successfully imprinted on the public mind that when someone met him for the first time it came as a shock and prompted involuntary exclamations that, understandably, wounded Alan's pride.

And this leads to a story. Alan was extremely sentimental. In September 1956, my wife, Mell, and I flew from Rome to Athens. We heard that Alan and Sue were staying at the Grand Bretagne Hotel, and we decided to run over and surprise them. When Alan opened the door we expected whoops, laughter—instead, he took one look at us, burst into tears, threw his arms around my neck, and sobbed. It took a minute before I could unpeel him with the plea that we were exhausted (we had just got in and hadn't even been to our own hotel room yet) and could he pour us a drink? He calmed down and poured the drinks, and we had a heartwarming reunion.

Later, back at the Palace Athenae, makeup man Henry Villardo brought us up to date on the cause of Alan's emotional outburst. Hating to travel, Alan had been coaxed away from his fortress, his home in Holmby Hills, to go to Athens to star in *Boy on a Dolphin* with some little-known Italian actress named Sophia Loren and to be guided by a director he didn't know. When he arrived, he found that the actress was several inches taller than he was and so bountifully equipped in features and figure that she was certain to make fifty percent of any two-shot a waste of film. Added to that, the director, Jean Negulesco, had already become quite interested in her. They had been shooting for six weeks under these unpromising conditions, with one more week to go, and Alan was miserable.

Mell and I departed Athens to tour Greece and met the Ladds several weeks later in Naples. Alan wasn't feeling good. He loved highly spiced food; his stomach did not. (He had had ulcers for years.) The result was many sleepless nights in pain. I don't doubt that his delicate digestion contributed to his early death.

Alan possessed to a high degree a quality that I've seen equaled by only two other stars: Rita Hayworth and Gary Cooper. None of the three were superb actors or technicians, but all had the ability to make a quite ordinary scene become—when projected on a screen—a thing of sensitive beauty and strength. I

believe that this gift was what made Alan the sensa-
tional screen star he was.

He was a good friend, and I valued that friendship. I
miss him very much.

It seemed that all of Hollywood wanted to make Lloyd's life hap-
pier. They rallied around at the December 12, 1981, *Autistic Children's
Telethon*, dedicating the event to his sixtieth anniversary in showbiz.
Hosting the telethon this year were Joe Campanella, Frankie Avalon,
Jack Klugman, and Gloria Loring.

Author Michael Schlossheimer, in his book *Gunmen and Gangsters*,
tells us about another project that needed Lloyd's expertise: "[Lloyd]
next appeared as a cantankerous oldster in the pilot for *Adam's House*,
a projected Karen Valentine series about a social worker. Besides being
funny, he is also touching as he opposes the demolition of his apartment building, describing his apartment's meaning to him and his late
wife. Those who saw Nolan break into tears knew this was more than
just acting. Once again, the actor was identifying with his role."

☆☆☆

Lloyd had known southern actress Virginia Dabney for many years.
They had worked together in the 1938 films *King of Alcatraz* and
Prison Farm, then again the next year in *The Magnificent Fraud*. Robert
Florey had directed both *King of Alcatraz* and *The Magnificent Fraud*,
and had fallen in love with Virginia. They wed in 1939 and enjoyed a
long, productive marriage until his death in 1979. She hadn't worked
in films since 1940, but had kept in contact over the years with many
of her friends in the industry, including, of course, Lloyd. Their rela-

Virginia Dabney (right) in her youth.
(From the collection of Rex A. Coughenour)

tionship was now intensifying and they were seeing each other in a different light.

The widow and widower had been alone long enough, and were now ready to remarry. On January 26, 1983, Virginia became Mrs. Lloyd Benedict Nolan and would be by his side for the rest of his life.

He sold his house and moved into hers.

In July, the couple went on a marvelous world cruise. Life was once again good.

But only for two more years.

CHAPTER 19
Time is Running Out

Vintage stars Lloyd, Virginia Mayo, and Dorothy Lamour appeared as themselves in a delightful 1984 episode of *Remington Steele* very appropriately entitled "Cast in Steele." As the less-than-competent Remington Steele, played by Pierce Brosnan, was trying to solve a murder, much-more experienced investigator Lloyd (hey, he'd played Michael Shayne, private eye, really well, after all!) gave him some pointers needed to find the evidence he was seeking. Lloyd was the only guest star given humorous lines, and he delivered them with much naturalness.

It was Woody Allen who provided Lloyd with his film swan song, *Hannah and Her Sisters*. The film, which stars Woody's live-in lover at the time, Mia Farrow played Hannah while Barbara Hershey and Dianne Weist played the sisters. Lloyd and Maureen O'Sullivan played their parents, Evan and Norma. (Ms O'Sullivan, in real life, was the mother of Mia Farrow.)

✩✩✩

Even though Lloyd had given up cigarettes a few years earlier, he was diagnosed with lung cancer in June. He kept this bad news to

Lloyd and Maureen O'Sullivan, playing aging Broadway stars, singing to their grandchildren in _Hannah and Her Sisters_ (Photographer - Brian Hamill)

himself as he arrived on the set to make a guest appearance on _Murder, She Wrote_. His co-stars sensed the truth, though. The show was an episode called "Murder in the Afternoon," in which he played an aging star of a soap opera. Lloyd had always had a poor memory, but it had gotten very bad now, and his physical strength was much diminished. Series star and old friend Angela Lansbury helped him greatly, having written into the script his reliance on cue cards, so he was able to fulfill this commitment.

Soon after, the time for hospitalization had come. Lloyd was admitted to Century City Hospital. Harvey Lapin visited him there, and came away feeling so sad. He knew then that his dear friend was dying. The hospital staff did all they could for him, but Lloyd had now accepted his fate and wanted to die at home. In mid-September, he was discharged from the hospital.

Two weeks later, on Friday, September 27, 1985, at 7:55 a.m., cancer won the battle. Lloyd died at the age of eighty-three.

His memorial service took place on October 1 at All Saints Episcopal Church in Beverly Hills. President Reagan sent flowers and a message to be read at the service. In attendance were about two hundred people, including Lloyd's *Julia* co-star Diahann Carroll, as well as his close friends. "I loved Lloyd like a father," says Harvey, who grieved much over the loss. "I was like his son."

Lloyd's body was cremated, and the ashes set to rest at Westwood Memorial Park in Los Angeles. His very simple grave marker bore his full name and a cross between the years of his birth and death.

Lloyd's final screen appearance on the small screen, the *Murder, She Wrote* episode, was aired six weeks later; *Hannah and Her Sisters* was released the following year. That, actor Wright King feels was writer/director Woody Allen's best film.

☆☆☆

"We'll miss him—and so will all autistic children."—*Variety*

"Nolan was to both critics and audiences the veteran actor who works often and well regardless of his material."—*Los Angeles Times*

"…he came to London to direct [*The Caine Mutiny Court Martial*] on stage and to act in the part he had made his own."—*The Times* (London)

Epilogue

Twice-widowed Virginia Dabney Nolan passed away on September 4, 1991.

In November, 2000, Melinda underwent knee surgery. The following day, a blocked artery suddenly and unexpectedly snuffed out her life. She was sixty. Left behind were her husband Tim, son Nolan, and daughter Miller.

Appendix
Known Works of Lloyd Nolan

STAGE

19?? – *Aristocracy*
1929 – *Cape Cod Follies*
1930 – *Sweet Stranger*
1931 – *Reunion in Vienna*
1932 – *Americana*
1933 – *One Sunday Afternoon*
1934 – *Ragged Army*
      Gentlewoman
1950 – *The Silver Whistle*
1951 – *Courting Time*
1954 – *The Caine Mutiny Court Martial*
1956 – *The Caine Mutiny Court Martial* (in London)
1960 – *One More River*

RADIO

1944 – *Lux Radio Theatre,* "Guadalcanal Diary" *Results, Inc.*
1951/2 – *Martin Kane, Private Eye*

FILM

1935 – *"G" Men*
       Stolen Harmony
       Atlantic Adventure
       She Couldn't Take It
       One-Way Ticket

1936 – *You May Be Next*
       Lady of Secrets
       Big Brown Eyes
       Devil's Squadron
       Counterfeit
       The Texas Rangers
       Fifteen Maiden Lane

1937 – *Interns Can't Take Money*
       King of Gamblers
       Exclusive
       Ebb Tide
       Every Day's a Holiday
       Wells Fargo

1938 – *Dangerous to Know*
       Tip-Off Girls
       Hunted Man
       Prison Farm
       King of Alcatraz

1939 – *Ambush*
       St. Louis Blues
       Undercover Doctor
       The Magnificent Fraud

1940 – *The House Across the Bay*
       Johnny Apollo
       Gangs of Chicago
       The Man I Married
       Pier 13
       The Golden Fleecing
       Charter Pilot

Michael Shayne, Private Detective

Behind the News

1941 – Mr. Dynamite

Sleepers West

Dressed to Kill

Buy Me That Town

Blues in the Night

Steel Against the Sky

1942 – Blue, White and Perfect

The Man Who Wouldn't Die

It Happened in Flatbush

Just Off Broadway

Manila Calling

Apache Trail

Time to Kill

1943 – Bataan

Don't Be a Sucker

Guadalcanal Diary

1944 – Resisting Enemy Interrogation (WWII training film, US Army, Air Corps)

1945 – A Tree Grows in Brooklyn

Circumstantial Evidence

Captain Eddie

The House on 92nd Street

War Came to America (narrator)

1946 – Two Smart People

Somewhere in the Night

1947 – Lady in the Lake

Wild Harvest

1948 – Green Grass of Wyoming

The Street With No Name

1949 – The Sun Comes Up

Bad Boy

Easy Living

1951 – The Lemon Drop Kid

1953 – Island in the Sky

Crazylegs
1956 – *The Last Hunt*
       Santiago
       Toward the Unknown
1957 – *Seven Waves Away*
       A Hatful of Rain
       Peyton Place
1960 – *Portrait in Black*
       Girl of the Night
1961 – *Susan Slade*
1962 – *We Joined the Navy*
1963 – *The Girl Hunters*
1964 – *Circus World*
1965 – *Never Too Late*
1966 – *An American Dream*
1967 – *The Double Man*
1968 – *Sergeant Ryker*
       Ice Station Zebra
1970 – *Airport*
1973 – *Normalization: A Right to Respect*
1974 – *Earthquake*
1975 – *The Sky's the Limit*
1977 – *Galyon*
       The Private Files of J. Edgar Hoover
1978 – *My Boys Are Good Boys*
1985 – *Prince Jack*
1986 – *Hannah and Her Sisters*

MADE-FOR-TV MOVIES

1967 – *Wings of Fire*
1973 – *Isn't It Shocking?*
1975 – *The Abduction of Saint Anne*
1976 – *The November Plan*
1977 – *The Mask of Alexander Cross*

Flight to Holocaust

Fire!

1979 – *Valentine*

1983 – *Adams House*

1984 – *It Came Upon the Midnight Clear*

TELEVISION GUEST ROLES

1950 – *The Ford Theater Hour,* "The Barker"

1952 – *The Ford Theater Hour,* "Protect Her Honor"

    What's My Line? (mystery guest, May 11th)

1954 – *The Arthur Murray Party,* April 12

1955 – *Climax!* "Sailor on Horseback"

    Ford Star Jubilee, "The Caine Mutiny Court-Martial"

    Toast of the Town (episode 9.3)

1956 – *MGM Parade* (episode 1.23)

1957 – *Playhouse 90,* "Galvanized Yankee"

    What's My Line? (guest panelist, December 29th)

    The Big Record (December 25th)

1958 – *Zane Grey Theater,* "The Homecoming"

1959 – *Wagon Train,* "The Hunter Malloy Story"

    Hallmark Hall of Fame, "Ah, Wilderness!"

    Westinghouse Desilu Playhouse, "Six Guns for Donagan"

    The Untouchables, "The George 'Bugs' Moran Story"

    Laramie, "The Star Trail"

    The Tennessee Ernie Ford Show (episode 3.24)

1960 – *Startime,* "Crime, Inc." (narrator)

    Bonanza, "The Stranger"

    The Barbara Stanwyck Show, "The Seventh Miracle"

    Zane Grey Theater, "Knife of Hate"

1961 – *Darrow the Defender* (unsold pilot)

    Bus Stop, "The Glass Jungle"

    General Electric Theater, "Star Witness: The Lili Parrish Story"

    General Electric Theater, "Call to Danger"

    Laramie, "Deadly Is the Night"

1962 – *The Dick Powell Show*, "Special Assignment"
    Laramie, "War Hero"
1963 – *The DuPont Show of the Week*, "Two Faces of Treason"
    The Great Adventure, "The Death of Sitting Bull"
    The Great Adventure, "The Massacre at Wounded Knee"
    Kraft Suspense Theatre, "The Case Against Paul Ryker" (parts 1 & 2)
    77 Sunset Strip (parts 1-5)
    The Virginian, "It Takes a Big Man"
    Pantomime Quiz, "Lloyd Nolan vs. Gisele MacKenzie"
1964 – *The Outer Limits*, "Soldier"
    Bob Hope Presents the Chrysler Theatre, "Mr. Biddle's Crime Wave"
    The Virginian, "The Payment"
1965 – *Daniel Boone*, "The Price of Friendship"
    The Bing Crosby Show, "What's a Buddy For?"
    Slattery's People, "Rally Round Your Own Flag, Mister"
1966 – *House Party* (September 15th)
1967 – *The Road West*, "A Mighty Hunter Before the Lord"
    Mannix, "The Name is Mannix"
    The Virginian, "The Masquerade"
1968 – *The Danny Thomas Hour*, "The Cage"
    Judd for the Defense, "The Devil's Surrogate"
    I Spy, "The Name of the Game"
1972 – *Owen Marshall: Counselor at Law*, "A Question of Degree"
    The Bold Ones: The New Doctors, "A Nation of Human Pincushions"
1973 – *McCloud*, "Butch Cassidy Rides Again"
    The F.B.I., "The Killing Truth"
1974 – *The Magician*, "The Illusion of the Curious Counterfeit" (part 2)
    Sandburg's Lincoln, "The Unwilling Warrior"
1975 – *Disneyland*, "The Sky's the Limit" (parts 1 & 2)
1976 – *Ellery Queen*, "The Adventure of the Sunday Punch"
    City of Angels, "The November Plan" (part 1)
1977 – *Gibbsville*, "The Price of Everything"
    McMillan & Wife, "Affair of the Heart"
    Police Woman, "Merry Christmas, Waldo"
1978 – *The Waltons*, "The Return"

Quincy, M.E., "A Test for Living"

The Hardy Boys/Nancy Drew Mysteries, "Search for Atlantis"

The American Film Institute Salute to Henry Fonda

1979 – *$sweepstake$* (episode 1.2)

1981 – *Archie Bunker's Place,* "Custody" (parts 1 & 2)

1984 – *Remington Steele,* "Cast in Steele"

1985 – *Murder, She Wrote,* "Murder in the Afternoon"

TELEVISION SERIES AS A REGULAR

1951-1952 – *Martin Kane, Private Eye*

1958-1959 – *Special Agent 7*

1968-1971 – *Julia*

RECORDINGS

1975 – *The American Spirit 1776-1976*

COMMERCIALS

1950s – The Jimmy Fund for Boston's Children's Hospital

1970s – Third National Bank

Public service announcement re autism

1980s – Poli-Grip denture adhesive

Bibliography

Books:

Gordon, Jeff. *Foxy Lady: The Authorized Biography of Lynn Bari*. Albany, GA: BearManor Media, 2010.

Henry, Marilyn and Ron DeSourdis. *The Films of Alan Ladd*. Secaucus, NY: Citadel Press, 1981.

Kanter, Hal. *So Far, So Funny*. Jefferson, NC: McFarland & Company, Inc., 1999

Schlossheimer, Michael. *Gunmen and Gangsters*. Jefferson, NC: McFarland & Company, Inc., 2002.

Magazine Articles:

Briggs, Colin, "Lynn Bari." *Classic Images,* December, 2009.

Curreri, Joseph, "The Name You'll Never Read in a Gossip Column." *TV Radio Talk,* April,

1969, pg. 36-38, 58-59.

De Roos, Robert, "The unforgettable man from many forgettable movies is proving unforgettable again." *TV Guide,* December 20, 1969, pg. 16-19.

Nolan, Lloyd, "The Role I Liked Best…" *The Saturday Evening Post,* March 11, 1946.

Nolan, Mell, "The Man I Married," *Silver Screen,* December, 1948.

Reid, James, "Good Bad Man." *Modern Screen,* March, 1937.

"TV Portrait Featuring Lloyd Nolan." *TV News,* April 18, 1952. Vol. 2, No. 41.

Vargara, John, "Quietly the Captain Waited," *Personality Parade,* October 26, 1954.

Wallace, Stone, "Lloyd Nolan, Hollywood's Nicest Tough Guy!" *Filmfax*

Newspapers:

Beverly Hills Press, "Actor Sells Apartments." March 24, 1955.

Hollywood Reporter, "Nolan's 50 years." December 6, 1977.

Hollywood Reporter, obituaries. January 21, 1981.

Los Angeles Daily News, "Movie Father Of Year." June 16, 1949.

Los Angeles Examiner, "Lloyd Nolan Building Sold." March 20, 1955.

Los Angeles Herald-Examiner TEMPO, "Travel," by Kit Snedaker. May 26, 1974.

Los Angeles Herald-Examiner TV Weekly, "Lloyd Nolan at 74—Avoiding Boredom," by Frank Torrez. March 20, 1977.

Los Angeles Times, "Lloyd Nolan Recalls Tragedy of Autism," by Ursula Vils. March 11, 1973.

Los Angeles Times, "Lloyd Nolan, the Actor's Actor, Dies," by Burt A. Folkart. September 28, 1985.

Los Angeles Times, "Postscript: Lloyd Nolan Will Host Telethon to Help Autistic Children," by Kris Lindgren. December 9, 1977.

New York Journal American, "Lloyd Nolan as Villain," by Dorothy Kilgallen. January 18, 1938.

New York Sunday News, "Lloyd Nolan." March 30, 1969.

New York Times, "Lloyd Nolan Is Dead At 83; Film, Theater and TV Actor," by George James. September 29, 1985.

The New Yorker, "New Laurels For Nolan," by Emory Lewis.

Pittsburgh Press, "Lloyd Nolan Bares Ordeal of Infantile Autism," by Ursula Vils. March 17, 1973.

San Francisco Chronicle, "Standford to Present Play Tonight." July 27, 1928.

San Francisco Chronicle, "Lloyd Nolan Here for Family Visit." June 17, 1934.

San Francisco Chronicle, "Few Actors Can Afford Stage, Says Nolan." November 10, 1935.

Variety, "Heston Will Present Honor To Lloyd Nolan." December 8, 1977.

Variety, obituaries. January 15, 1981.

Online Resources:

Erickson, Hal. "All Movie Guide." www.allmovie.com

"Internet Movie Database." www.imdb.com.

"Jay Nolan Community Services, Inc." www.jaynolan.org

McCarthy, Dennis. "It's Not Perfect, But Kids Don't Care." www.thefreelibrary.com.

Other Resources

Lloyd Nolan Oral History, SMU, #109, dated July 28, 1976. Interviewer Dr. Ron-
       ald J. Davis. Included with collections of the Margaret Herrick Library in
       Beverly Hills, CA.

Index

About The Authors

Joel Blumberg has made a career out of two of his favorite interests: sports and classic films. For over three decades, he was a radio sportscaster in his native New York. He was involved in NFL football, Major League Baseball, NHL hockey, and both the NBA and NCAA college basketball. In addition, he has been a movie buff since childhood. While working for radio station WGBB, he was able to launch his radio program Silver Screen Audio, which has been on the air since 2004 and on the web at www.silverscreen-audio.com. On the program, he has interviewed many of the stars of the golden age. He has also done commentary and produced special features for several DVDs.

Joel, his wife Jill, and daughter Miranda live in East Meadow, New York.

Sandra Grabman has authored three previous biographies: *Spotlights & Shadows: The Albert Salmi Story* (2004); *Plain Beautiful: The Life of Peggy Ann Garner* (2005); and *Pat Buttram, the Rocking Chair Humor-*

ist (2006). Then she teamed up with retired actor Wright King to pen a book about the era of live television from the actors' perspective, entitled *No Retakes!* (2008). *Classic Images* magazine has deemed *Spotlights & Shadows* "Best Book of the Year 2004" and *No Retakes!* "Best TV Book of the Year 2008." In biographies, it's the off-screen life of her subjects that interests Grabman the most. She feels that there's something important to learn from everyone's life story.

Sandra and hubby Roy have two grown sons and two really short cats.

Breinigsville, PA USA
08 October 2010
246958BV00004B/4/P